VOLUME 1

CONSOLIDATED
B-24 LIBERATOR

BY FREDERICK A. JOHNSEN

Distributed by:
Airlife Publishing Ltd.

500 114 920 05

Copyright © 1996 Frederick A. Johnsen

Published by
Specialty Press Publishers and Wholesalers
11481 Kost Dam Road
North Branch, MN 55056
United States of America
(612) 583-3239

Distributed in the UK and Europe by
Airlife Publishing Ltd.
101 Longden Road
Shrewsbury
SY3 9EB
England

ISBN 0-933424-64-7

940.
544
973

500114920

All rights reserved. No part of this book may be reproduced
or transmitted in any form or by any means, electronic or
mechanical including photocopying, recording or by any
information storage and retrieval system,
without permission from the Publisher in writing.

Material contained in this book is intended for historical and
entertainment value only, and is not to be construed as usable
for aircraft or component restoration, maintenance or use.

Designed by Greg Compton

Printed in the United States of America

TABLE OF CONTENTS

THE CONSOLIDATED B-24 LIBERATOR

PREFACE

While it may be true that more aluminum was used to build B-24 Liberators than any other American aircraft of World War Two, the same cannot be said for the amount of printer's ink devoted to books about the Liberator line. The appetite for more and more published material about Liberators and Privateers remains unabated, and this premier volume in the WarbirdTech Series is a seasoned entree in the smorgasbord.

This volume is designed as a book with its own vantage point, as well as being a worthy adjunct to other B-24 works. At the risk of appearing self-indulgent, let me suggest this volume as a useful complement to *B-24 Liberator— Combat and Development History of the Liberator and Privateer* which I wrote for Motorbooks International in 1993. Both books contain different pieces of the B-24 historical puzzle. As a research aid, some photo captions in this volume contain bibliographic references to other B-24 books where more photos of the same specific topic may be found. The WarbirdTech Series assumes a level of interest on the part of readers who will respond to the use of technical art and manual excerpts to uncover the workings of the

Newly made and gleaming with potential, B-24J-145-CO posed for the camera. This San Diego-built Liberator (identified in the nomenclature block letters CO) retained a Motor Products nose turret and inward-retracting nosewheel doors. (SDAM)

B-24J-90-CO 42-100294 with braced pitot masts on forward fuselage and extra fuel tanks in bomb bays. (SDAM)

Liberator line. This is an exciting venture that goes more than skin deep to chronicle important aircraft.

As you read this volume, the history of the B-24 and PB4Y as machines will hopefully provide a glimpse into the lives of the men and women who built and crewed these aircraft. If the Liberator and Privateer are icons of World War Two, it is because they were animated by creative engineers, skilled craftsmen, and plucky crews. The story of the B-24 is a mixture of art, science, and human fortitude that far transcends the ingots of aluminum borrowed from the earth to build the aircraft. As we salute the Liberator line, let us respectfully pay tribute to all the men and women who built,

flew, and maintained Liberators and Privateers, and who, by so doing, gave us worthy role models.

Many individuals and organizations graciously made materials and expertise available to assist with this book. They include: Peter M. Bowers, Paul J. Bruneau, John and Donna Campbell, Bert Creighton, George W. Cully, Jeff Ethell, Charlie Glassie, Jr., Todd Hackbarth, Henry B. Harmon, Leonard S. Horner, Sharon Lea Johnsen, Don Keller, Keith Laird, Tony Landis, Gerald Landry (California Institute of Technology 10-foot Wind Tunnel), William T. Larkins, The Liberator Club (and George Welsh), Ray Markman, Bob McGuire, Dave Menard, Bill Miranda, Jim Morrow, L.M. Myers, Matthew E. Rodina, Jr., San Diego

Aerospace Museum (and Ray Wagner), Ron Sathre, Carl Scholl (Aero Trader), David Tallichet, David D. West, and others. As you view the photography in this book, remember the efforts of company and military photographers, largely unrecognized, whose photographic records offer a priceless glimpse into the past.

Photo caption abbreviations used in this book include SDAM for San Diego Aerospace Museum collection and AFM for Air Force Museum.

FREDERICK A. JOHNSEN
1996

THE LIBERATOR DEFINED

When the XB-24 first lifted from San Diego's runway on December 29, 1939, it embodied Consolidated Aircraft's vision of a warplane; a super bomber riding on a promising new airfoil. Though subsequent combat information pointed up vulnerabilities in early Liberators, the intent was obvious: The B-24 was a serious bombardment airplane possessing great range and load-carrying capability.

The Liberator was a proactive response from Consolidated Aircraft when asked by the Air Corps in 1938 to consider building Boeing B-17s under contract. After inspecting the Boeing product in Seattle, Consolidated's corporate view was ambitious, yet succinct: A totally new Consolidated product could be designed and built in the same amount of time it would take to adapt the existing B-17 to production in San Diego. Consolidated's Frank Fink was given the task of fleshing out a mock-up of the proposed bomber in January 1939, before it had been designed. The key points were incorporation of the promising Davis airfoil and the basic wing planform of the Model 31 flying boat, the use of four PBY-style engine packages, and the use of two bomb bays, each of which could match the B-17's single bay for capacity.[1] The twin tails of the Model 31 also came into play; in fact, for the first flight of the XB-24, the tail assembly was literally removed from the Model 31 and placed on the Liberator; subsequently, greater span was introduced on Liberator horizontal surfaces, but the Model 31 influence remained.[2]

Before the first flight of the XB-24, wind tunnel tests confirmed the new Davis high-lift airfoil offered greater range than a National Advisory Committee for Aeronautics alternate that Consolidated tested in the same planform. But the value of the wing employed by the B-24 may have

In December 1942 a Royal Air Force Liberator III or IV (B-24D variants) paused at Boeing Field, Seattle, Washington, in the heart of Flying Fortress country. (Peter M. Bowers collection)

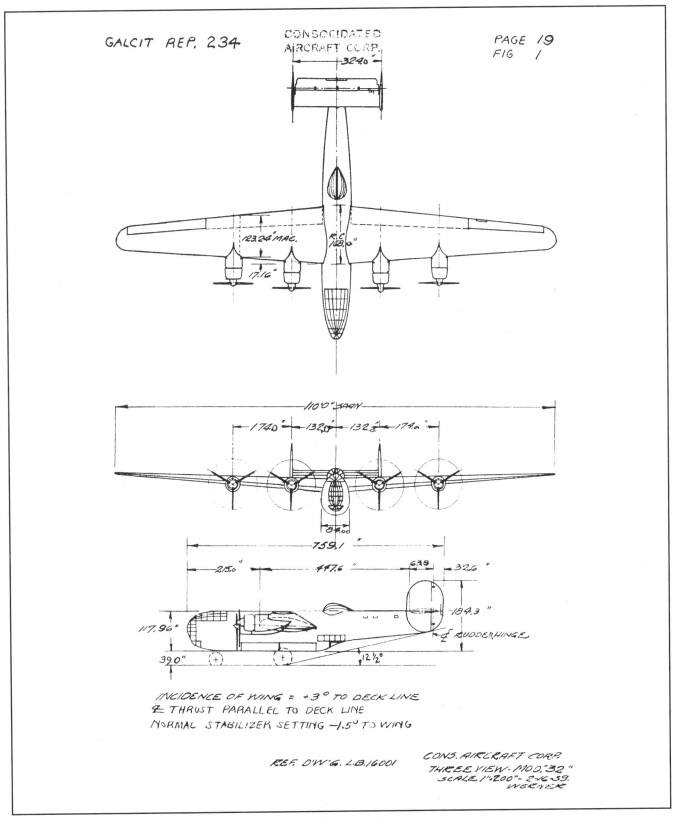

Metamorphosis of the Liberator before the first aircraft was built is evidenced by a three-view drawing of Consolidated Aircraft's Model 32 as tested in the Cal Tech (GALCIT) wind tunnel between 16-20 February 1939. Bulbous fuselage with stepped ventral area bears little resemblance to the real XB-24, but 110-foot wing planform and twin tails point the way to the Liberator line. (Consolidated drawing courtesy California Institute of Technology GALCIT wind tunnel)

been helped by other features as well as by the shape of the airfoil itself. The high aspect ratio (wide span with relatively narrow chord, or front-to-back measurement) is an inherent efficiency when used with other airfoils as well as the Davis. Also, the wide spacing between the front and rear spars in the wing selected for the B-24 enabled Consolidated engineers to devise ample fuel storage—another way of assuring greater range. When Consolidated designers pinned their hopes on the Davis wing with the high aspect ratio for the B-24, they got performance, albeit possibly with the caveat that some pilots found it more difficult to master the subtleties of flying the Davis wing effectively compared to other airfoils. Other design features of the B-24 correctly telegraphed the future of aviation, replacing the B-17's tailwheel with a tricycle gear design, and using Fowler area-increasing flaps instead of the B-17's split flaps, in an era when designers were embracing new concept at all the manufacturing plants.

The U.S. Army Air Corps issued type specification number C-212 in February 1939 to cover the proposed Consolidated design; Martin and Sikorsky were afforded nominal times to submit competing designs, but this was in essence a formality. Within a few weeks, on February 21, 1939, the Consolidated proposal was forwarded to Washington for approval. The contract that bought the XB-24 was signed on March 30, 1939; the prototype Liberator flew a day under nine months later—a tribute to Consolidated's ingenuity and determination.

Liberators were in the war right from the start, when a B-24A, number 40-2371, was destroyed on the ramp at Hickam Field during the December 7, 1941 bombing of Hawaii by the Japanese. During the first year of war for the United States, B-24s of the USAAF were dispatched to the Pacific, the Middle East, England, and the Aleutians.

Some numbered air forces flew both B-24s and B-17s in 1942, and up through the end of the war, this was the case in Europe. But a conscious decision saw the number of B-24s sent to the Pacific increase and totally replace remaining B-17s by 1943, while in England the Eighth Air Force ultimately re-equipped some B-24 bomb groups with new B-17s.

LB-30 Liberators, built to British specifications but retained by the USAAF after Pearl Harbor was bombed, saw combat in the Pacific in early 1942, and by June of 1942 in the Aleutians. Surviving LB-30s flew Panama Canal protection patrols into 1944.

B-24Ds, with extensively glazed greenhouse noses, operated out of the middle east with the HALPRO Detachment beginning in the summer of 1942. That year, China was bombed by Liberators for the first time. The global use of B-24s was established early in the conflict, and remained to the very end.

In many ways, development and production of B-24s during World War Two illustrated textbook examples of logistical problems inherent in that modern war. Liberators on the production line often lacked modifications dictated by rapidly-changing combat situations. As with many warplanes of the era, it was expedient to continue building somewhat deficient Liberators quickly, and then route the new bombers through modification centers set up to apply the latest armament and equipment changes. That way, production lines could remain productive while institutional changes to the basic Liberator design were folded into the process in a more orderly fashion. This does not mean the assembly lines were frozen; a look at Liberators

Royal Air Force Liberator G.R. VI, number KH258 carries SNAKE legend on waist, indicating aircraft has been configured for Southeast Asia operations. (Ken Sumney via SDAM)

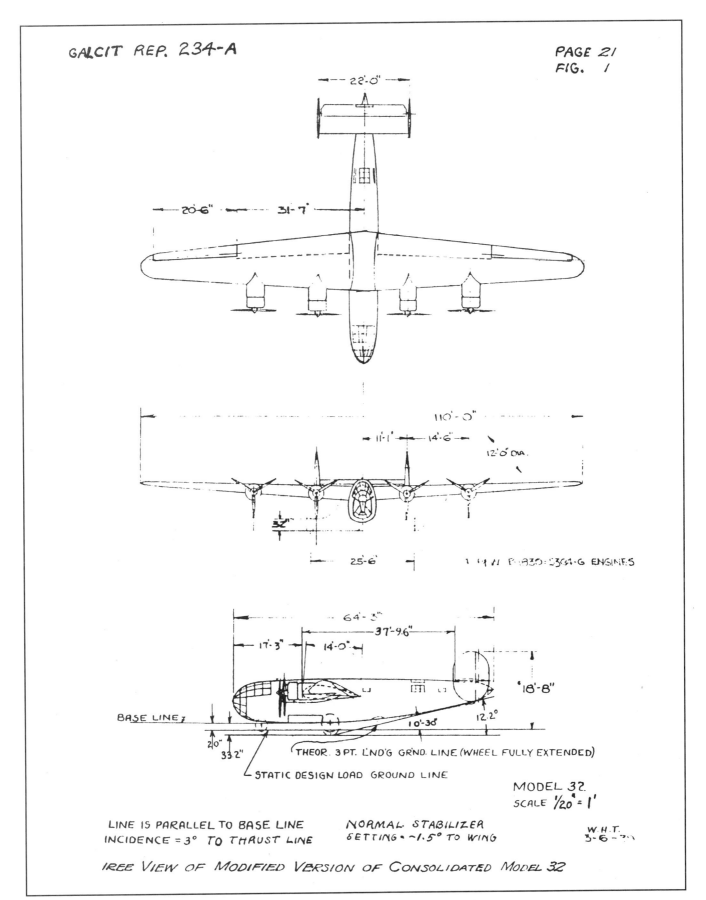

By mid March 1939, a modified Model 32 fuselage joined the classic wing and tail in the wind tunnel at Cal Tech.

from the various assembly plants reveals an ongoing metamorphosis. But the modification centers were vital for their ability to respond quickly to change orders, and to customize Liberators for specific theaters of operations or specialized missions.

Literally tons of weight were added to the basic B-24 design throughout the Second World War as the realities of combat demanded heavy armaments and armor. Crew accommodations were revised, especially for the bombardier and navigator in the narrow nose, to better allow them to do their jobs accurately. The Liberator weight and performance changes are illustrated by data for the pre-war B-24A and the last full-fledged

	B-24A	B-24M
SPAN/LENGTH	110'/63'9"	110'/67'2"
EMPTY/GROSS WT.	30,000/53,600 lbs.	36,000/64,500 lbs.
SPEED AT ALTITUDE	292MPH/15,000ft.	300MPH/30,000ft.[3]

production Liberator, the B-24M, as shown in the chart above.

The weight figures are telling: The B-24A was expected to heft not quite 12 tons in excess of its empty weight, while the B-24M, with an empty weight already three tons heavier than the A-model, was tasked with lifting more than 14 tons over its empty weight. That works out to more than five tons additional weight for the B-24M than envisioned for the B-24A, still riding on the same basic Davis wing. Pratt and Whitney R1830 radial engines of 1,200 horsepower apiece powered all Liberators; upgrades and turbosupercharging enhanced performance of later models. Interestingly, range for the A-model was 2,200 miles; for the B-24M, it was 2,100 miles.

[1] Allan G. Blue, *The B-24 Liberator*, Charles Scribner's Sons, New York, 1975 (pp. 11-12). [2] Conversation, author with Ray Wagner, San Diego Aerospace Museum archivist, February 1996. [3] Gordon Swanborough and Peter M. Bowers, *United States Military Aircraft Since 1908*, Putnam, London, 1971.

Last Liberator built at San Diego was B-24M-45-CO 44-42722, construction number 6658. Emerson nose turret appears to have removable protective coating on Plexiglas, allowing metal and micarta parts to be sprayed silver with no fear of resultant overspray. (SDAM)

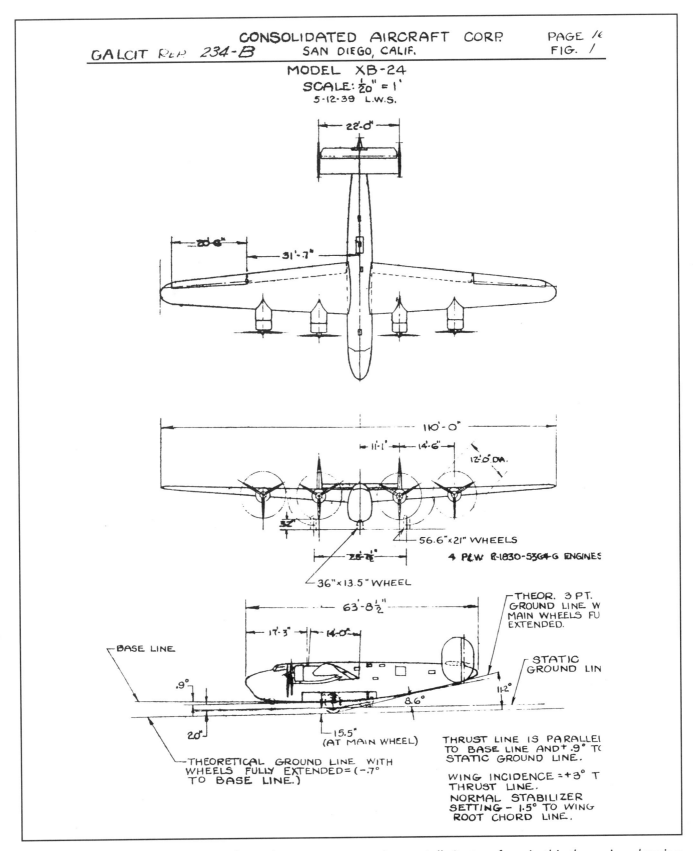

CONSOLIDATED AIRCRAFT CORP.
SAN DIEGO, CALIF.

PAGE 16
FIG. 1

MODEL XB-24
SCALE: 1/20" = 1'
5-12-39 L.W.S.

22'-0"

20'-6"
31'-7"

110'-0"
11'-1"   14'-6"
12'-0" DIA.
32"
56.6" × 21" WHEELS
4 P&W R-1830-53G4-G ENGINES
25'-4½"
36" × 13.5" WHEEL

63'-8½"
17'-3"   14'-0"
THEOR. 3 PT.
GROUND LINE W
MAIN WHEELS FU
EXTENDED.

BASE LINE
STATIC
GROUND LIN
.9°
11.2°
8.6°
20°
15.5"
(AT MAIN WHEEL)
THEORETICAL GROUND LINE WITH
WHEELS FULLY EXTENDED = (-.7°
TO BASE LINE.)

THRUST LINE IS PARALLE
TO BASE LINE AND +.9° TC
STATIC GROUND LINE.

WING INCIDENCE = +3° T
THRUST LINE.
NORMAL STABILIZER
SETTING - 1.5° TO WING
ROOT CHORD LINE.

Tested at Cal Tech from 16-22 May 1939, the XB-24 presented essentially its true form in this three-view drawing reproduced in a wind tunnel report. For its first flight, the XB-24 borrowed, literally, the horizontal and vertical tail surfaces removed from the Model 31 flying boat. Later, a horizontal tail of greater span was instituted for the Model 32 Liberator. (Via Cal Tech wind tunnel)

LIBERATOR 2 EVOLUTION

B-24s used in Europe typically evolved with more armor, both metallic and glass, than their Pacific counterparts, due to the nature and concentration of German flak and frontal fighter attacks. This resulted in a weight penalty for Liberators assigned to European USAAF operations.

In the tropics, crews were more willing to discard heavy powered tail turrets in favor of light open-air tail gun mounts, while over frigid Europe in winter at altitude, this was not a favored choice.

Even the stereotype of massed strategic formations of Liberators must be scrutinized, for the USAAF record shows Liberators were also employed in single-ship strikes, at low- to medium-altitude, often against tactical targets including individual bridges and cargo ships. (The distinctions between tactical and strategic bombardment become even more blurred when considering the use of Liberators against Japanese merchant shipping, since the Japanese relied on a spidery network of ships to haul

Late Ford B-24M with both pilots' escape hatches and command deck hatch aft of wing open. This M-model was photographed on the Hawthorne, California, airport circa 1946. Faired-over top turret opening and faded star on wing suggest this Liberator entered the surplus market. It may have been a training aid at a technical school. (Northrop photo)

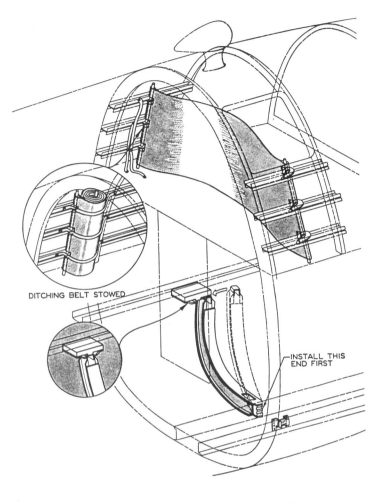

DITCHING BELT STOWED

INSTALL THIS
END FIRST

Ditching belt provided a safety restraint for those crew members who congregated on the B-24 command deck aft of the wing in the event of a water landing. Late Liberators were fitted with an escape hatch on the top right side of the command deck. Another late revision was the use of bomb bay stiffeners, as depicted in this page from the Liberator pilot's handbook.

Figure 48B — Ditching Belt and Bomb Door Stiffeners Installation

Revised 25 April 1945   RESTRICTED   65

Command deck ditching hatch is visible on Ford B-24M-20-FO 44-51228 displayed at Lackland AFB, Texas. Extra patches are scars from this aircraft's test career.

CONSOLIDATED
B-24 LIBERATOR   13

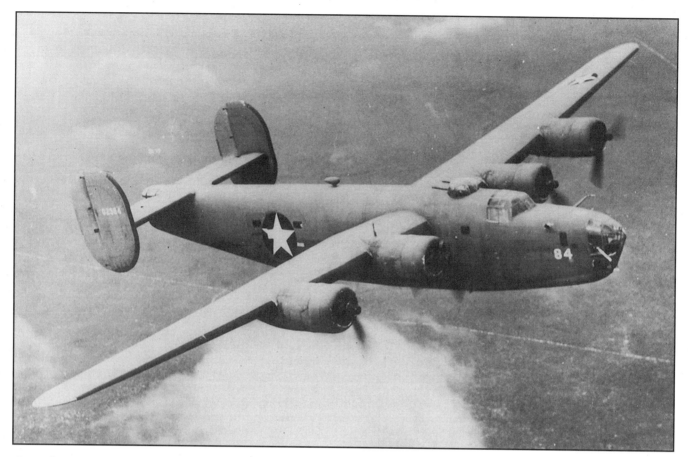

One of nine B-24Cs (40-2384) was used extensively in tests of Liberator modifications at Eglin Field, Florida. Visible on right inboard engine nacelle is radio antenna mast. (Liberator Club)

vital raw materials to Japan, making the sinking of even a single freighter an event of some strategic consequence.)

Throughout World War Two, Liberators or Privateers fought in every theater of operations, often exceeding intended gross weights, and performing tasks beyond those envisioned when the design was created in 1939. It is difficult and potentially misleading to categorize an aircraft with as many versatile facets as the Consolidated Liberator. Production changes affected many parts of the B-24, and came at a pace so rapid that some of the evolutionary chain of the Liberator line has been obscured. Twists in the construction of Liberators and Privateers include the following:

SOMETHING BORROWED

Evidence in tech orders suggests that Consolidated Aircraft, with a history of building multi-engine seaplanes, frugally used its previously-developed designs to benefit the Liberator and Privateer. The B-24 was Consolidated Model 32. A large number of parts used in the construction of B-24s are labeled with the prefix 32. The PB4Y-2 Privateer (Consolidated Model 100) likewise incorporated many obviously identical Model 32 parts in its construction. Popular Liberator history books have long reported the B-24 used the same twin-tailed vertical fins and rudders as did Consolidated's experimental Model 31 flying boat. A B-24D/J Airplane parts Catalog (the Dash-4 tech order) dated 1

December 1944 corroborates this, by listing many parts of the B-24's vertical fin with the part number prefix 31. Of further note, incidental parts in the rudders of B-24s carried part numbers beginning in 29—the model number of Consolidated's four-engine PB2Y Coronado flying boat. Still other B-24 parts bore the prefix 28, suggesting they originated in the design of the Consolidated Model 28 PBY Catalina.

LONG OR SHORT ENGINE COWLING DICTATED PROPELLER BLADE WIDTH

The ring cowling on classic wide oval B-24 engine nacelles was shortened during B-24D and E-model production. This had the effect of giving more clearance for propeller blades in the fully-feath-

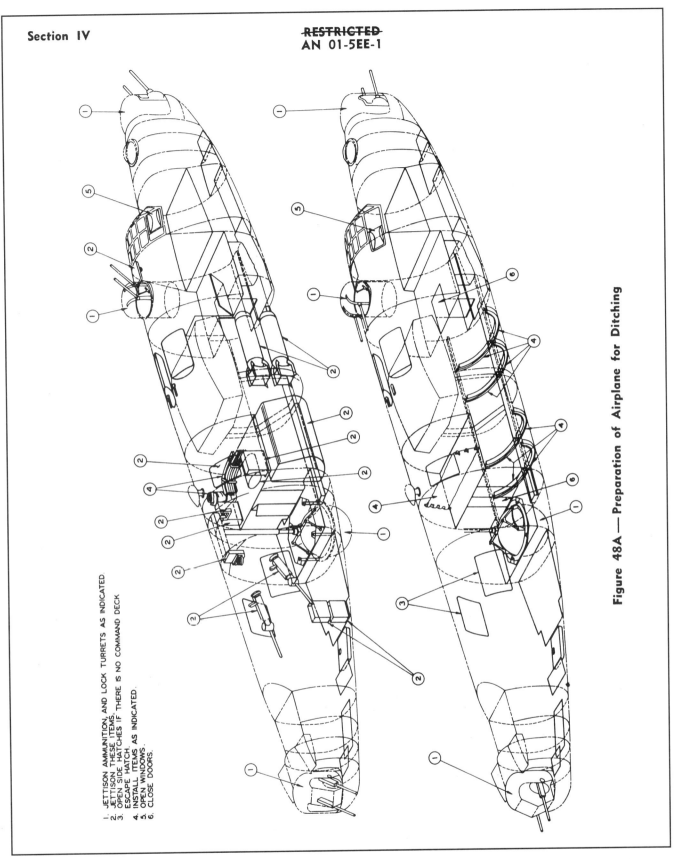

1. JETTISON AMMUNITION, AND LOCK TURRETS AS INDICATED.
2. JETTISON THESE ITEMS.
3. OPEN SIDE HATCHES IF THERE IS NO COMMAND DECK
   ESCAPE HATCH.
4. INSTALL ITEMS AS INDICATED.
5. OPEN WINDOWS.
6. CLOSE DOORS.

Figure 48A — Preparation of Airplane for Ditching

Top (left) drawing from late-war Liberator pilot's manual depicts a B-24 in flight before ditching preparations are made; bottom (right) drawing shows same aircraft with loose items jettisoned, ditching hardware installed, and turrets stowed and locked in neutral position.

ered position on the short-cowled aircraft. In a practical sense, the short cowlings permitted the use of wider Hamilton-Standard 6477A-0 paddle blades in place of the Hamilton-Standard 6153A-18 or 6353A-18 "toothpick" propeller blades of earlier B-24s. (Toothpick blades could, however, be installed on short-cowled B-24s.)

According to a May 10, 1944, revision to the B-24 Erection and Maintenance manual, "Short ring cowling was installed on B-24D airplanes beginning with 41-23970 except for six numbers, 42-63751 to 42-63757, inclusive. The latter had long cowling. B-24E airplanes 41-28409 to 41-28416, inclusive, and 42-6976 to 42-7005, inclusive, have long cowling. All other B-24E and all B-24G, H and J airplanes use short cowling."

SELF-SEALING TANKS HELD LESS OIL

Each engine nacelle of the B-24 housed an oil tank. Prior to B-24D serial number 41-23719, each tank had a capacity of 39 U.S. gallons. With the addition of self-sealing liners on 41-23719 and subsequent B-24s, capacity diminished to 32.5 U.S. gallons per tank, as the Liberator became more combat-survivable.

COWL FLAPS CHANGED SIZES

According to the B-24 Erection and Maintenance manual, at least three variations on cowl flap lengths existed. These were subject to change during engine overhauls, and therefore aircraft serial numbers soon lost meaning as a way to differentiate which B-24s used which cowl flaps. Early B-24Ds were equipped with nine-and-a-half-inch cowl flaps which were adjusted to allow all eight flaps to open to a maximum of 30 degrees, and allow the flaps to close to within three or four degrees of the nacelle cowl tangent line in the fully closed position.

Desert sand-colored B-24D with early flat navigator top window instead of astrodome also has radio masts on both inboard engine nacelles; whip antenna ahead of direction finding 'football' antenna on fuselage.

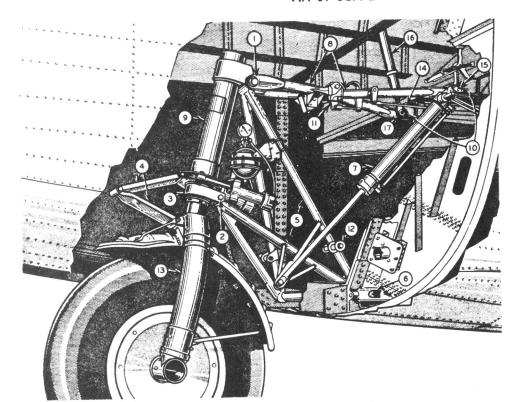

1. Bolts
2. Bolts
3. Lower Collar
4. Torque Links (Scis
5. Two "V" Struts
6. Pivot Shafts
7. Hydraulic Jack
8. Drag Link Assemb
9. Oleo Strut
10. Airplane Structure
11. Latch
12. Door Actuating R
    Assemblies
13. Oleo Fork
14. Latch Linkage
15. Shaft
16. Booster Spring
17. Shaft

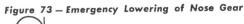

Figure 73 — Emergency Lowering of Nose Gear

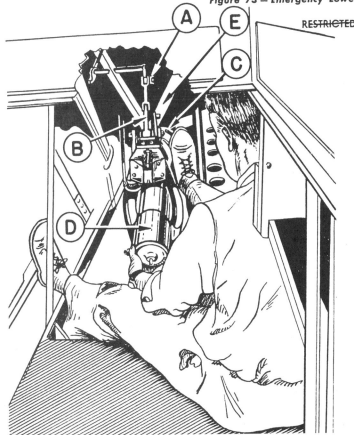

RESTRICTED

1. Remove curtains by pulling out pins in top of two aft curtain cables, unfastening curtain from floor beams, and pulling out pins in top of two forward curtain cables.

2. Remove latch linkage release pin "A" by pushing in against spring, revolving locking tab to line with pin, and pulling out. (Re-insert in disconnected link to avoid losing pin.)

3. Pry open latch "B" with fingers or screwdriver.

4. Sit under flight deck on the floor. Place right foot on shimmy damper collar "C" and place both hands under top of oleo strut "D."

5. Push with right foot and lift with both hands to extend nose gear.

6. After nose gear is in "DOWN" position, push up on drag strut "E" and press latch into gear locked position, if latch has not already been engaged.

Emergency extension of Liberator nose gear was a drafty manual process as depicted in technical order excerpts.

Later, B-24D, E, G, and H-model Liberators were fitted with 11-inch cowl flaps. On some D- and J-models, the cowl flaps were shortened to 10 inches. The cowl flap jacks were adjusted to allow a maximum opening of only 22 degrees (plus or minus one degree), with a closed position of two and a half degrees, plus or minus a half degree.

Production cowl flaps then settled on the 10-inch length on B-24Gs, B-24Hs, and B-24Js. These production 10-inch installations provided differential maximum opening angles, with the top flaps opening to only 12$\frac{1}{4}$ degrees, while the four lower cowl flaps opened to 22 degrees, with a tolerance of plus or minus one degree on all these cowl flaps.

(The evolution of differing B-24 cowl flap lengths and opening characteristics may coincide with

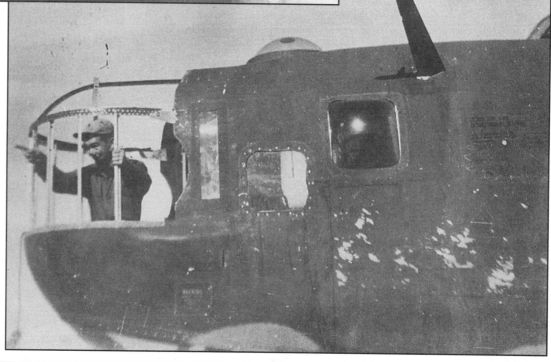

To improve field of vision for navigators and bombardiers, some 15th Air Force B-24s had nose turret replaced with aluminum-framed Plexiglas greenhouse. This Liberator also has been fitted with a variety of 15th Air Force nose windows for the same purpose. (Charlie Glassie Jr. collection)

WARBIRDTECH
S E R I E S

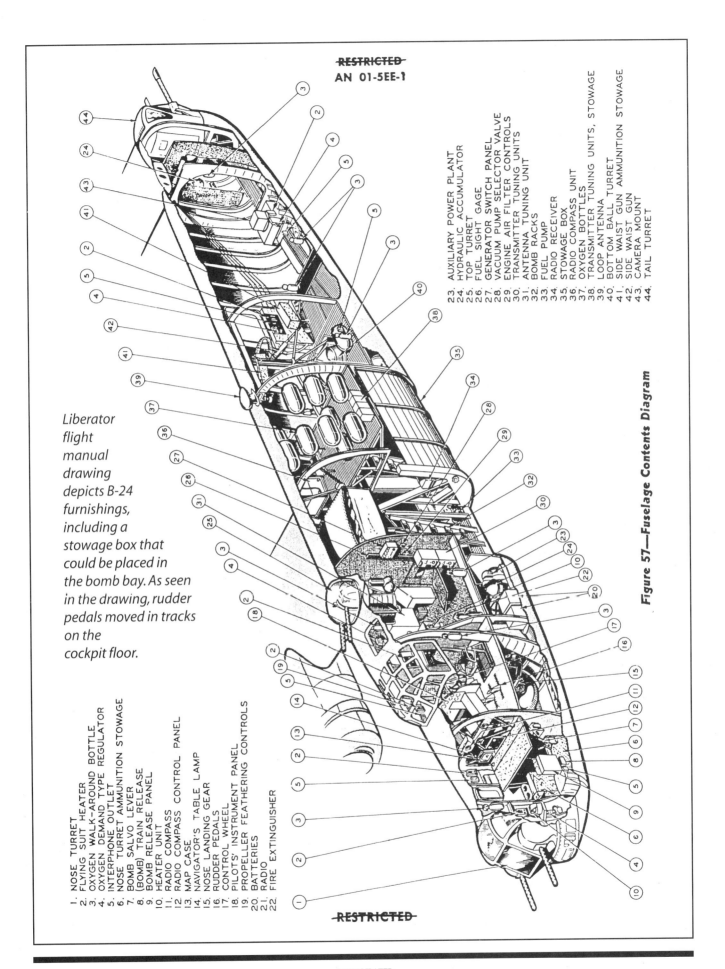

Figure 57—Fuselage Contents Diagram

Liberator flight manual drawing depicts B-24 furnishings, including a stowage box that could be placed in the bomb bay. As seen in the drawing, rudder pedals moved in tracks on the cockpit floor.

1. NOSE TURRET
2. FLYING SUIT HEATER
3. OXYGEN WALK-AROUND BOTTLE
4. OXYGEN DEMAND TYPE REGULATOR
5. INTERPHONE OUTLET
6. NOSE TURRET AMMUNITION STOWAGE
7. BOMB SALVO LEVER
8. (BOMB) TRAIN RELEASE
9. BOMB RELEASE PANEL
10. HEATER UNIT
11. RADIO COMPASS
12. RADIO COMPASS CONTROL PANEL
13. MAP CASE
14. NAVIGATOR'S TABLE LAMP
15. NOSE LANDING GEAR
16. RUDDER PEDALS
17. CONTROL WHEEL
18. PILOTS' INSTRUMENT PANEL
19. PROPELLER FEATHERING CONTROLS
20. BATTERIES
21. RADIO
22. FIRE EXTINGUISHER

23. AUXILIARY POWER PLANT
24. HYDRAULIC ACCUMULATOR
25. TOP TURRET
26. FUEL SIGHT GAGE
27. GENERATOR SWITCH PANEL
28. VACUUM PUMP SELECTOR VALVE
29. ENGINE AIR FILTER CONTROLS
30. TRANSMITTER TUNING UNITS
31. ANTENNA TUNING UNIT
32. BOMB RACKS
33. FUEL PUMP
34. RADIO RECEIVER
35. STOWAGE BOX
36. RADIO COMPASS UNIT
37. OXYGEN BOTTLES
38. TRANSMITTER TUNING UNITS, STOWAGE
39. LOOP ANTENNA
40. BOTTOM BALL TURRET
41. SIDE WAIST GUN AMMUNITION STOWAGE
42. SIDE WAIST GUN
43. CAMERA MOUNT
44. TAIL TURRET

Consolidated efforts to stop a tail buffeting problem that early Liberators suffered in some cowl flap settings.)

TURBO CONTROLS CHANGED

Turbosupercharger waste gate controls were four lollipop handles on the left side of the throttles on all B-24Ds and B-24Es, as well as early B-24Gs, Hs, and Js. These four handles were cable-linked to hydraulically-operated waste gate regulators. In later G-, H-, and J-models (and other later models), electronic turbosupercharger regulators were installed, resulting in a selector dial on a box mounted on the control pedestal in the former location of the lollipop handles. (Non-turbosupercharged PB4Y-2 Privateers

A Middle-East B-24D assigned to a 9th AF unit crumpled onto splayed landing gear, circa 1943. Aircraft number 38 is repeated on vertical fins. 'Toothpick' propellers on engines 3 and 4 were turning as they hit the ground, bending all three blades and suggesting that side of the aircraft went down first.

WARBIRD**TECH**
SERIES

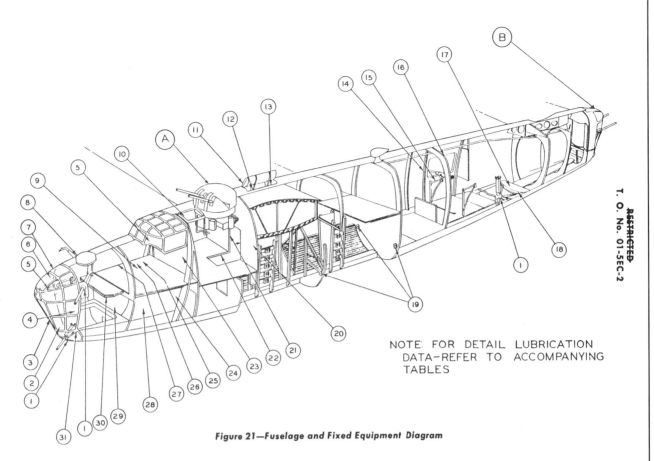

NOTE: FOR DETAIL LUBRICATION
DATA—REFER TO ACCOMPANYING
TABLES

Figure 21—Fuselage and Fixed Equipment Diagram

Key
No.   *Part to Be Lubricated*

1. Machine gun swivel sockets..........................
2. Nose ventilator..
3. Windshield wiper (outside hinge joints)..............
4. Bombardier's seat (all friction points)..............
5. Windshield anti-icer pumps. ....
6. Windshield wiper converter (Zerk)...................
7. Windshield wiper flexible drive shaft (inside)...........
8. Bombardier's escape hatch hinges....................
9. De-icer control handle...............................
10. Emergency exit hatch latch and hinges...................
11. Life raft cradle hinges...............................
12. Life raft cradle ejecting mechanism...................
13. Life raft cradle release mechanism...................
14. Side gunner's wind deflectors (all friction points).......
15. Side gun swivel mounts...............................
16. Side gunner's hatch latches and hinges..................
17. Camera mount hinges.................................
18. Rear entrance hatch latches and hinges..................
19. Bomb bay door drive sockets.........................
20. Vacuum four-way valve...............................
21. Radio compartment aft sliding door tracks..............
22. Radio compartment trap door hinges...................
23. Radio operator's seat (all friction points)..............
24. Gear boxes for nose wheel doors (3 Zerk fittings each)...
25. Pilot's and copilot's seats (all friction points)...........

26. Seat tracks...
27. Ventilators...
28. Nose wheel doors (8 Zerk fittings)....................
29. Servo control unit (pressure fitting at front of wheel well)
30. Nose wheel door emergency opening handles...........
31. Bomb release levers (all hinge points).................

Technical manual drawing of B-24D shows items requiring lubrication. Structural bulkhead beltframes are shown. This B-24D is configured with single flexible .50-caliber machine gun in ventral hatch opening, instead of later ball turret.

350
TURRET
MUNITION
300
50. CAL
RDS. THIS
24 TOHAM
RD BLOCK 15

PULL
TO OPEN

T-13429

Interior right side of aft fuselage of a B-24L-15-FO shows rigid ammunition feed chutes leading to tail guns from wooden box at left of photo. Ventral crew hatch is in open position in the photo. (Air Force photo via SDAM)

had a flat aluminum plate covering the place on the pedestal where either type of control would have been mounted.)

C-87 GREW

The first C-87 Liberator Express transport models of the B-24 were 65 ft., 10½ in. long, with the rear of the fuselage ending in a blunt cap initially capable of mounting a flexible machine gun for defense. Beginning with C-87 number 41-11605, the length was increased to 68 ft., 5⅜ in., due to a tapering tail cone extension that provided more streamlining.

FUEL CELL VENTING CHANGED

On Liberators prior to the B-24J, fuel cell venting was located in the fuselage above the wings. On J-models, the opening for each of the two wing fuel vent systems was located in the wings, outboard of station 5.0 on each side of the airplane. (The change on J-models may account for the fact raised vent fairings are visible on many photos of B-24Js and later models, but not earlier Liberators.) To vent the wing cavity around the rubber fuel cells, air scoops were mounted on the wing upper surface aft of the inboard nacelles.

A vent tube extended from the rear spar at station 5.0 downward and out of the aft end of the inboard engine nacelles. Beginning with B-24G number 42-78075 and B-24J number 42-73390, the outlet of these vent tubes was relocated about 40 inches inboard of the inboard nacelles to place the outlet away from engine exhaust gases.

CONTROL WHEEL HOUSING CHANGED

In early Liberators, from LB-30s, through the handful of B-24Cs, and up through B-24D number 41-11938, inclusive, the housing for the push-pull control wheel column was essentially triangular in shape, with the broad surface on top. Subsequent B-24s had a rectangular housing around the control columns. These distinctions are visible in some B-24 cockpit photos, and, along with other clues like turbosupercharger control styles, can reveal information about the age of the aircraft.

Free-blown bombardier's side blister was added to a number of B-24Ls and Ms destined for the 15th Air Force to improve lateral view; aircraft in photo is a B-24L-15-FO. (SDAM)

WING FLAPS WARPED

Because of the taper in planform and cross section of the B-24's Davis wing, the Fowler area-increasing flap in each wing had to be warped to ensure a continuous fit in conformity with the underside of the wing. On B-24C aircraft and B-24Ds up to, but excluding, number 40-2350, warping the flaps was accomplished by creating differing rigging tensions between the inboard and outboard operating cables. According to the B-24 Erection and Maintenance manual, "This differential ranges up to 130 pounds, depending on each individual flap and airplane."

On B-24Ds numbers 40-2350 up to, but excluding, 41-11754, the flaps were built with greater reinforcement, making warping via differential rigging tension not always feasible. For these Liberators, the Erection and Maintenance manual noted: "…a larger inboard forward stop is provided and should be used, if necessary, to reduce the amount of warping required. The trailing edge of the flap will trail aft of its normal position at the inboard end on installations using the longer stops."

Beginning with B-24D number 41-11754, the wing flaps were constructed with the chord plane already warped one-and-a-half degrees to fit the wing contour. This eliminated the need for extreme rigging tension differential, although a moderate differential might still be needed to ensure a snug fit.

A FLARE FOR PYROTECHNICS

B-24Cs and B-24Ds up to number 41-11587 carried a set of signal equipment including one A-1 portable signal container, nine signals (type M-10 or M-11), one M-2 signal pistol, and one A-1 pyrotechnic pistol holder.

Later Liberators could be outfitted with 4.5-inch reconnaissance flares. A fixed flare chute in the floor, behind station 4.1, was provided on airplanes previous to B-24D number 41-24090, according to the Erection and Maintenance manual. The flares were stowed in strap hangers in a vertical position on the right side of the fuselage and a horizontal array on the left side of the fuselage, just forward of the side gunners.

Beginning with B-24D number 41-23640, a container for a dozen day or night drift signals was placed on the upper right side of the fuselage above the rear entry hatch.

On B-24D 42-40138 and subsequent aircraft, the signal equipment package consisted of a standard army equipment package that included one A-7 signal flare container assembly, one M-8 signal pistol and mount, 12 type A-6 signal flares, and one A-2 pyrotechnic pistol holder.

MAIN GROUPS OF B-24 STYLES

A 20 September 1945 revision to the B-24 Dash-1 Pilot's Flight Operating Instructions defined three main categories for B-24 production under the headings Group I, Group II, and Group III. According to these instructions, "This group designation is necessary to distinguish the 'G' and 'H' models from the 'J' model. The distinguishing features of the 'J' model are the C-1 Autopilot and M-7 bomb sight which replace the A-5 automatic pilot and S-1 bomb sight of the 'G' and 'H' models. The 'G' and 'H' models also differ from the 'J' model in respect to fuel, armament, and other equipment." Restated, the manual said: "All Group I and early Group II airplanes are equipped with the type A-5 automatic pilot. Later Group II and all Group III airplanes are equipped with the type C-1 Autopilot."

The Flight Operating Instructions also explained: "Model B-24L airplanes (late Group III) are basically Model B-24J airplanes with hand-held twin tail guns replacing the power-driven tail turret of the 'J.'

Model B-24M airplanes (late Group III), also basically Model B-24J airplanes, can be identified by the centralized fuel control system and the SAC-7 tail turret which replaces the hand-held gun installation on Model B-24L airplanes."

Some late Group III airplanes relocated the navigator from the cramped nose of the B-24 to the rear of the flight deck.

Later-model Group III B-24s were equipped with an all-electric bomb release system using A-4 bomb rack release devices.

COCKPIT ESCAPE HATCHES

According to a revision to the B-24 Pilot's Handbook dated 18 December 1945, some late Group II B-24s were equipped with two emergency overhead exits above the pilot and copilot. (Late Group II Liberators include Ford B-24Ms, some of which used revised cockpit canopies with knife-edge windscreens and overhead hatches.) According to the manual, "The

hatches are opened by pulling outboard on the handles at the inboard edge of the hatch. The hatches may be held in a partly open position by using the hooked rods on each end of the hatch opening. These exits are to be used only with the engines stopped, when the airplane is on the ground following a crash landing, or in a forced descent on water (DITCHING)."

COMMAND DECK ESCAPE HATCH

Late Consolidated and Ford B-24s, including Ford B-24Ns, had an additional escape hatch in the upper right side of the command deck, immediately behind the wing. This was to be used in ditching. (This appears to be on the opposite side of the command deck from the location of an escape hatch installed in some Indian Air Force B-24s, presumably by Hindustan Aircraft Industries after the war. Likewise, PB4Y-2 Privateers had an upper aft escape hatch installed.)

Twin Bell E-11 recoil adaptors with oversized grips on the outboard sides cradled the .50-caliber guns of the lightweight B-24L tail gun position. Booster motors helped feed the ammunition from flexible chutes into the guns. (SDAM)

SINGLE TAILS FOR THE AIR FORCE

DESIGN CHANGES TRANSFORM LIBERATOR INTO A LIVELIER BOMBER

The single-tail B-24N built by Ford amalgamated the best Liberator design changes into a bomber that promised to remedy several key complaints levied against earlier B-24s. The large single rudder had more authority, and was better able to cope with two engines out on a side than was the twin-tail of most B-24s. This conventional single-tail arrangement enhanced lateral stability of the B-24. The revised canopy of the N-models (seen also on some Ford-built B-24Ms) improved the pilots' view by reducing the number of ribs between clear-view panels. This new knife-edge windscreen was part of a revision that also saw overhead escape hatches put in the cockpit to facilitate pilot egress. (One suggestion made for production B-24Ns was to eliminate the traditional dorsal hatch near the top turret, because the cockpit

Single-tail Ford XB-24N used simplified canopy with openable escape hatches above pilots. Flat window in place of bulging astrodome gave pilots better forward visibility. Stub for mounting horizontal stabilizers had no dihedral; stabilizers did. (Ford via Yankee Air Museum)

WARBIRDTECH
SERIES

XB-24N (44-48753) used tail gun emplacement employing aluminum sphere mounting two .50-caliber guns, with sighting station in Plexiglas blister beneath rudder. (SDAM)

Hooded B31 turbosuperchargers are seen as black silhouettes beneath cowlings of the XB-24N. Hood increased airspeed. (SDAM)

XB-24N was fitted with enclosed waist guns in K-7 mounts; Emerson 128 nose turret gave better nose contour than earlier Emerson A-15 in twin-tail Liberators. (Peter M. Bowers collection)

escape panels made it redundant.) And the new Emerson Model 128 spherical nose turret, tested earlier in a twin-tail B-24G, was said to improve the Liberator's speed and handling because of its improved streamlining, over other nose turrets like the Emerson A-15 and Motor Products/Consolidated designs. Servo tabs on the control surfaces of the "N" made control forces lighter than on previous Liberators—another feature welcomed by pilots. The revamped B-24N promised to rectify problems that had grown like parasites on B-24s through the crush of wartime expedients that saw the traditional Liberator's design burdened with weight and drag concessions.

The desirability of a single tail for B-24s was stated succinctly in an Army Air Forces Proving Ground report in April 1944 that evaluated the first AAF single-tail Liberator,

the XB-24K. In part, the report concluded: "The handling characteristics of the B-24K model are excellent. The rudder and elevator controls are a great deal more sensitive than in the conventional model and should alleviate pilot fatigue." The report continued: "The performance of the 'K' model with two engines out on one side is decidedly superior to that of the standard B-24 airplane. Comparatively little change in rudder trim is necessary for straight and level flight."

Additionally, the XB-24K afforded large increases in the fields of fire for the ball turret, waist guns, top turret, and tail turret, the report noted. The report, signed by Col. C.B. Overacker, chief of the proof department at the Eglin Field AAF Proving Ground Command facility, recommended a single tail similar to that of the XB-24K "be incorporated in all future production B-24 aircraft."

Another Eglin test report from August 1944 highlighted benefits derived from the installation of the spherical Emerson Model 128 turret in the modified nose of a B-24G. The resulting nose contours on the adapted G-model closely resembled the lines of the Ford XB-24N. The report concluded: "The all-around performance, especially during formation flying, of the B-24G with the subject nose turret, is greatly superior to that of any B-24 of the G, H, or J series which has been tested at this station.... The superior performance of this airplane can be attributed largely to the Emerson 128 ball turret installation in the nose." Visibility for the bombardier and navigator were found to be better with the Emerson 128 installation than with standard B-24s. Side windows afforded bombardiers the ability to look aft, watching bomb impacts, and the side view was said to be

Muzzles of .50-caliber guns in retracted ball turret are visible ahead of tailskid on XB-24N. (AFM)

YB-24N-FO 44-52056 traveled between a number of stateside bases before being reassigned from Air Materiel Command to reclamation in November 1947.

Two YB-24Ns went to Keesler Field, Mississippi, site of training schools, before being consigned to scrap at Kingman, Arizona. Aircraft in photo at Keesler is either YB-24N 44-52053 or 058, both of which were sent to that base. (81 TRW/HO)

adequate for even short approaches from 90-degree angles to the target run. Pilot visibility was enhanced by the smoother contours of the modified nose in this test airplane. (In a standard nose-turreted B-24, the turret protruded above the normal nose contour, obstructing the pilots' view forward.) Testers did comment on the excessive number of canopy frames in the otherwise-unchanged B-24G cockpit—a hindrance that would be corrected on the B-24N.

B-24 pilots sometimes spoke about the Liberator's "step," meaning a particular cruise attitude that was desirable to attain, and was achieved, they said, by climbing above desired cruise altitude and diving slightly to gain speed, and set the aircraft "on the step." According to the test report of the modified B-24G with the Emerson 128 nose turret, a standard B-24J used for comparison "was extremely sluggish and hard to maintain 'on the step' at air speeds of 158 to 160 MPH. The B-24G handled very well and was much easier to keep "on the step" at that speed.... Operating with a full military load, the B-24J type aircraft becomes unmanageable in close formation at air speeds of 155 MPH or less. Although the handling characteristics of the (modified) B-24G left much to be desired at similar speeds, they were a decided improvement over those of the B-24J."

In these two 1944 Liberator tests, validation was found for two major design innovations built into the Ford B-24N: A single tail and the Emerson 128 spherical nose turret. In addition to better handling and working arrangements for the crew, all the changes poured into the XB-24N, including the use of R-1830-75 engines, were said to give this variant 300 miles more range than any other nose-turreted B-24, when all were flown at maximum cruise power with a 5,000-lb. payload.

In December 1944, a letter from

YB-24N 44-52057 was sent to Chanute Field, another technical training location, before being scrapped at Kingman. Of interest is nose number 144. YB-24Ns used A-6D lightweight tail turret similar to conventional B-24s. (AFM collection)

Progenitor of USAAF single-tail Liberators was B-24ST (later XB-24K) made by Convair at San Diego; refined N-model was built by Ford in Willow Run, Michigan. (Air Force photo)

USAAF headquarters in Washington, D.C., signed for Gen. Hap Arnold by Brig. Gen. Frederic H. Smith, Jr., the deputy chief of air staff, described B-24 developments this way: "For the past year much pressure has been expended on the B-24 program in an effort to develop a really combat worthy airplane. The results are now becoming apparent. The XB-24N received its initial flight recently and is now at Wright Field undergoing performance tests. Upon completion of the work at Wright Field, it goes to Eglin Field for operational suitability tests and it is planned shortly thereafter to fly this airplane to the United Kingdom for... inspection and comments. By this action the theaters reaction to the airplane may be obtained in time to make any required changes before production is too far along. This is essential, because modification facilities for the B-24 are almost non-existent." The letter continued, acknowledging the Liberator's legendary versatility: "B-24 modification facilities have recently been greatly curtailed by the accelerated B-29 program, and due to the fact that the B-24 has so many diversified functions, those modification centers still available are completely overloaded."

A couple weeks after General Smith's letter, a 30 December 1944 message routed to General Spaatz from General Arnold advised: "Installation of Bell Power Boost mount in nose of B-24K by CVAC (Consolidated Vultee Aircraft) Tucson (Ariz.) was 90% complete today." This was a cleaned-up version of the Bell mount earlier adapted to a B-24H in England, and flown to the United States for evaluation. General Arnold clarified nomenclature of single-tail

Late configuration of the XB-24K sported a Convair version of an Eighth Air Force-devised nose, with Bell gun mount. (SDAM)

Photos of the XB-24K tail show a remarkable similarity to the original single tail first fitted to the PB4Y-2 Privateer (bottom). XB-24K rudder trim tab changed from the time of the 1943 photo (right) to a larger tab at the top of the XB-24K rudder in the inset photo. Original Privateer single tail used same essential aerodynamic shape already proven on the K-model, with high-mounted trim tab. Visible changes on Privateer are hinges and a slight rounding to the bottom trailing edge of the rudder. Production Privateers subsequently heightened vertical fin with a cap, and relocated rudder trim tab to bottom trailing edge. Then, the evolved Privateer rudder was adopted for the single-tail XB-24N. It is reasonable to conclude Convair capitalized on its single-tail research, leap-frogging from the XB-24K to the PB4Y-2, and lending designs to the B-24N. (Air Force, SDAM, and Todd Hackbarth collections)

Liberators for General Spaatz, adding: "B-24K with single tail and Emerson ball nose is now designated the B-24N. Estimate arrival date of prototype 1 March 45 in your theater." (This message referred to the B-24K modified with a Bell twin gun mount, that was distinct from the B-24N with the Emerson ball in the nose. Both developments were watched anxiously by USAAF planners in Europe. There is no evidence to suggest either the XB-24K or any B-24N reached Europe in 1945.)

In January and February 1945, ongoing message traffic between HQ USAAF, Eighth AF, and 15th AF documented a search for a late-model B-24 configuration that would satisfy the needs of both Eighth and 15th Air Forces. A February 12, 1945, message from General Arnold anticipated the production of B-24Ns for combat as it spoke about configuring B-24Ls for Europe: "The B-24N will soon

Seemingly a photo of an airplane that never existed, this YB-24N carries serial number 44-52052, one digit lower than traditional lists of YB-24N serials. This number at one time had been assigned to a Ford B-24M, but this allocation was later changed to the N. A USAAF monthly armament chart dated 1 August 1945 does list B-24N-1-FO serials ranging from 44-52052 through 52059—one more aircraft than most rosters indicate. As of November 1993, the Air Force historical archives which contain record cards for Air Force aircraft had no listing for any aircraft bearing serial 44-52052. Theories about this aircraft range from a numbering mistake that may later have been corrected by Ford or the Air Force, to the possibility Ford never delivered this aircraft to the USAAF. (Yankee Air Museum via Todd Hackbarth)

View looking forward through XB-24N Emerson 128 nose turret shows external flexible ammo chutes and power cables. Welded tube structure overhead helped support turret. (Convair photo via SDAM)

replace the B-24L in production and such changes that cannot be readily incorporated in the B-24L will probably be incorporated in the B-24N aircraft." On February 17, 1945, General Spaatz asked General Arnold to dispatch a B-24N to the European Theater of Operations and Mediterranean Theater of Operations as soon as possible to allow Eighth and 15th Air Force representatives to come to an agreement on how to configure N-models jointly. The actual end of fighting in Europe was less than three months away, and still the need for B-24Ns was apparent to USAAF planners in February 1945, who could not afford crystal-ball hunches about when their war would end.

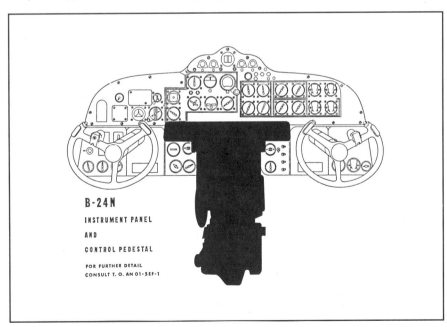

Ford B-24N instrument panel showed major shift in Liberator panel design. Dark area is control pedestal containing engine levers and trim tab wheels.

Popular history says the AAF's XB-24K and B-24N single-tail Liberator variants were independently derived, with no common ground shared with the Navy's PB4Y-2 Privateer. While this probably pertains in the realms of research and rationale, some commonality exists between the B-24N and the PB4Y-2 tail construction that bears noting.

Liberator historian Allan Blue reported the switch of a rudder from an RY-3 with that of an errant B-24N in an effort to divine the cause of a minor controllability vexation in the N-model. The U.S. Navy's RY-3 used the same tall tail as the PB4Y-2; the movable rudder assembly obviously was interchangeable with that on the shorter-finned B-24N.

When Convair built the PB4Y-2 Privateer for the Navy, the company changed its model designation from Model 32, as used on Liberators, to Model 100 for the Privateer. Yet since the Privateer incorporated substantial Liberator components, many parts in the Privateer still bore the signature Model 32 prefix to their numbers. This includes portions of the single-tail dorsal fin and attach fittings on the Privateer.

The use of Model 32 prefixes on these Privateer single-tail parts is strong evidence to suggest the company was wisely conserving costs by using common parts to create the single tails wanted by each service. In fact, the three prototype XPB4Y-2 Privateers were converted from twin-tail Liberators,

Vertical tail of XB-24N shared some commonality with Navy PB4Y-2. Photo was probably taken on the Ford flightline. (SDAM)

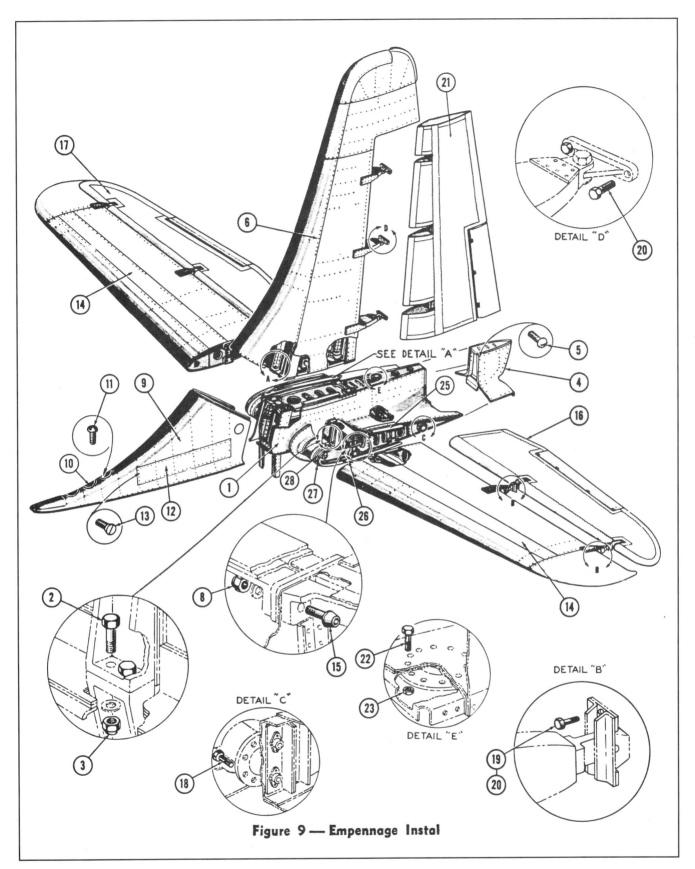

Figure 9 — Empennage Instal

Privateer parts catalog drawing shows single-tail pieces, including dorsal fin, stub assembly for attaching vertical fin and horizontal stabilizers, some elevator parts, and tail turret fairing, which carry Model 32 part numbers elsewhere in the catalog, suggesting some commonality with USAAF single-fin B-24 designs.

The XB-24N flew to San Diego where engineers investigated apparent rudder anomalies, at one point switching rudders with an RY-3 transport offshoot of the Privateer. Dark rudder trim tab visible in photo possibly could be a painted Privateer component. Style of tail numbers was changed on XB-24N. (SDAM)

and, according to Blue's research, one USAAF Eighth Air Force unit was in the process of converting a twin-tail B-24 to single-tail configuration when the end of hostilities halted the project. Convair had, according to Blue, designed the single-tail attach fittings for the horizontal and vertical stabilizers to be compatible with a standard Liberator fuselage, making such swaps feasible.

If the Air Force and the Navy had distinct and separate research and development of their single-tail Liberators and Privateers, it is rea-sonable to assume Convair frugally found a way to make some hardware common to the needs of both services.

TO THE "NTH" DEGREE

In July 1944, a decision was made to deliver Liberators from Convair/San Diego, Ford/ Willow Run, and North American/Dallas without tail armament, which would be customized at modification centers for specific theater-of-operations dictates, according to historian Blue. Though this scheme was short-lived, it briefly gave rise to an earlier Liberator being desig-nated B-24N, at least on paper; the North American Liberators to be delivered without tail armament. This paperwork exercise should not be confused with the Ford single-tail B-24N.

In fact, a Convair B-24 performance chart printed in 1944 lists B-24Ns, but shows them fitted with the wrong engines to be the Ford product; no doubt this was a reference to conventional North American-produced Liberators. North American stopped making Liberators in 1944, and the N-

model nomenclature was applied to the single-tail Ford product.

AAF Pilot Got "N" Off the Ground

Army Air Forces pilot Stephen D. McElroy, who retired as a brigadier general, was a plant representative at the Ford Willow Run, Michigan, Liberator assembly line. He recalled in an interview that the first flight of the XB-24N was lagging, due at least in part to a question over pay for the Ford company test pilots. This slowed the N-project, McElroy explained. Finally, McElroy took paperwork for the XB-24N and signed for it, as AAF plant representative. Next, as official custodian of this now-AAF property, McElroy said he made the first flight in the XB-24N, rather than wait for resolution of issues concerning the company pilots.

Tail Turret Reversion on YB-24N

The sole XB-24N used a tail gun position with two .50-caliber machine guns protruding from a small bulbous metal fairing, located below a bulging sighting window for the gunner. The seven YB-24Ns used the late-model A-6D (company designation SAC-7) tail turret from Southern Aircraft Corporation. This was a conventional-looking B-24 tail turret that was lightened from earlier SAC and Motor Products variants.

B-24N Nearly in Combat?

Deployment of B-24Ns—probably meaning the handful of YB-24N service-test variants completed by Ford—almost happened in 1945, according to B-24 crew commander then-Capt. Leonard Horner. Horner's crew and eight others were groomed stateside for low-altitude night bombing of Japanese shipping, relying on H2X/LAB (Low Altitude Bombing) radar bomb aiming equipment. Horner recalled: "The mission was to stooge around in the dark at 500 feet and drop on anything that wasn't ours. It was really accurate...."[1]

In November 1945, two months before being consigned for scrap, the XB-24N looked like this, still bearing its dark rudder trim tab. Visible in nose anti-glare panel is notch characteristic of Ford B-24s. (William T. Larkins photo via John Campbell)

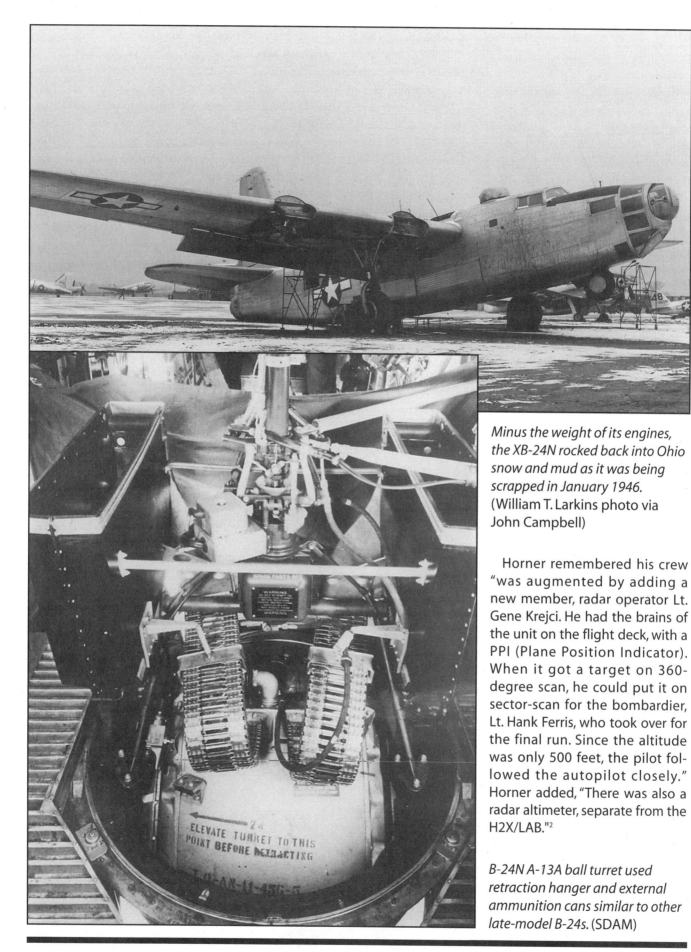

Minus the weight of its engines, the XB-24N rocked back into Ohio snow and mud as it was being scrapped in January 1946. (William T. Larkins photo via John Campbell)

Horner remembered his crew "was augmented by adding a new member, radar operator Lt. Gene Krejci. He had the brains of the unit on the flight deck, with a PPI (Plane Position Indicator). When it got a target on 360-degree scan, he could put it on sector-scan for the bombardier, Lt. Hank Ferris, who took over for the final run. Since the altitude was only 500 feet, the pilot followed the autopilot closely." Horner added, "There was also a radar altimeter, separate from the H2X/LAB."[2]

B-24N A-13A ball turret used retraction hanger and external ammunition cans similar to other late-model B-24s. (SDAM)

"After finishing six weeks training at Langley (Virginia), we were sent by train to Savannah (Georgia)… where we picked up brand-new B-24Ns," Horner said. "We got perhaps eight hours shakedown and transition, during which the pilots and copilots discovered and loved the mechanical servo tab control surfaces that made the N-model lighter on control force. Otherwise, there was no flying difference that I noticed, other than the usual continuous revision of instrument panel layout."[3]

Time arrived for the handful of B-24N crews to deploy, and they were given orders to depart in flights of three aircraft on three successive days, their gear loaded in bomb bay racks for the migration to Karachi, India, and thence to points unknown, Horner said. While Horner was tapped to lead the second flight, the first element of three B-24Ns departed at sunrise, only to be recalled back to Savannah, and all the N-models waited until the crews were ordered to fly them up to Langley. Upon arrival at Langley, the pilots and copilots were sent to Fort Worth, Texas, for transition training into Consolidated's big B-32 Dominator, instead. The remainder of the crews were given two weeks' leave during the pilot/copilot transition to B-32s, ultimately rejoining the pilots for full-crew B-32 tactics training, Horner said, before VJ Day put an end to that. Thus combat for the B-24N faded.

[1] Letter, Lt. Col. Leonard Horner, USAF (Ret), to Frederick A. Johnsen, 8 October 1993.
[2] Response by Lt. Col. Leonard Horder, USAF (Ret), to questionnaire from Frederick A. Johnsen, October 1993.
[3] Letter, Lt. Col. Leonard Horner, USAF (Ret), to Frederick A. Johnsen, 8 October 1993.

The single-tail XB-24N, embodying a host of Liberator refinements, promised to be the ultimate B-24 for combat until peace rendered it excess. In October 1944, the XB-24N was photographed at the Ford plant having its compass calibrated. (Brig. Gen. Stephen D. McElroy collection)

AIRBORNE GAS STATION

Years before Boeing introduced the highly successful flying boom method of aerial refueling, the British pioneered an operational way of transferring gasoline from one aircraft to another in flight that today seems hopelessly archaic, and, optimistic. Nonetheless, the British system, which enabled BOAC Liberators to span the Atlantic while carrying useful loads, was a milestone in its day.

A seldom-seen offshoot of the British system was tested by the USAAF in 1943 as a possible means of extending the range of bombers—the same tactic employed so successfully by the postwar Air Force. In fact, the AAF tests originated from a 1942 concept that called for bombing Japan from Wake Island, but, according to a USAAF test summary, "the project was abandoned because the equipment was not developed quickly enough." (Army Air Forces Board Project No. [T] 9—Tactical Application and Test of Refueling in Flight of Heavy Bombardment Aircraft, 10 March 1944.) It is perhaps no coincidence that the chosen receiver aircraft for the tests was a B-17—shorter in range than a B-24—while a spacious B-24D served as the tanker. However, the testers did note: "The receiving system may be installed in other type aircraft such as the B-24, but the modification is considerably more complex than on the B-17."

The tanker was B-24D 40-2352; the receiver was B-17E 41-2539. The B-24D carried extra bomb bay fuel tanks, and a bomb bay-mounted reel stowing the refueling hose. The B-17E featured a rear-facing refueling receptacle in a blister on the right side of the aft fuselage near the tail gun emplacement.

Connecting the B-24 tanker with the B-17 receiver was accomplished by having the B-17 trail a 250-foot steel hauling cable with a 25-pound sinker weight and a pawl grapnel (containing a bayonet fitting to attach to the refueling hose) on the end. According to an appendix to a USAAF Materiel Command Engineering Division report on test results at Eglin Field, Florida, the B-24 formated with the trailing B-17 cable "at a point approximately 130 feet to the rear and one wingspan to the right of the receiver. Upon reaching this position the tanker fires a projectile which carries a light cable across, and impinges on, the hauling line." The B-24 tanker's line was attached to a four-pronged hook, which was to cross over the B-17's trailing line and snag the sinker and grapnel at the end. By retracting the B-24's line, the B-17's steel cable was brought aboard the Liberator, where the weight and grapnel were removed, exposing the bayonet fitting to which the B-24's refueling hose

B-24D tanker number 40-2352 refueled B-17E over Eglin Field in 1943. (Air Force photo)

was then attached. The appendix noted: "While the receiver reels in the hauling line to which the hose is attached, the tanker is paying out the hose and maneuvering to a position approximately 75 feet above and 75 feet to the right of the receiver. After the nozzle is engaged by the four toggles within the coupling, the system is flushed with CO_2 (carbon dioxide) following which fuel is transferred. When the fuel has been passed, the system is once again flushed with CO_2 following which the receiver releases the nozzle amidst a stream of methyl bromide as an added fire preventative." (Appendix II—Operation of the Flight Refueling Equipment During Flight Tests at Eglin Field [MX-204], USAAF Materiel Command Engineering Division, 20 July 1943.)

The Liberator's position during refueling was such that the B-24 pilot could observe the B-17E's number four (outboard righthand) engine beneath him, with the B-24 cockpit "approximately straight above the trailing edge of the B-17E's right wing," according to a

B-17E number 41-2539 had fairing beside tail gun emplacement for refueling receptacle. Plate on gun muzzles held mirror enabling observer in gunner's position to see refueling receptacle during tests. (Air Force photo)

USAAF memorandum report on the refuelings. The tanker B-24 used for the tests did not have a bulged pilot's side window, but the testers noted, "it is believed that a blister would cause too much distortion and, therefore, do more harm than good…" It was found difficult to hold the B-24 in this refueling position for extended periods of time, "and after about 10 minutes in this position the pilot begins to feel very fatigued. However, since the entire refueling takes only 12 to 13 minutes in this position (not counting contact and separation operations), it is not considered objectionable." (Army Air Forces Materiel Command Flight Section Memorandum Report on Pilot's Comments on Refueling Project [B-24D], ENG-19-1609-A, June 18, 1943).

The test crews measured a transfer rate as high as 1,450 gallons of gasoline in 13 and a half minutes over Eglin Field. The installation of the flight refueling gear (essentially the same as that used by Britain's Flight Refueling, Ltd.) was performed by Pennsylvania Central

Portions of hose, reel, and line devices are visible in the bomb bay of B-24D tanker 40-2352. (Air Force photo)

Airlines, with subsequent modifications taking place during flight testing at Eglin. Extra refueling tankage in the Liberator totaled 1,720 gallons held in eight tanks: One in the right front bomb bay, a small tank over the hose reel drum in the left front bomb bay, two more tanks in the rear bomb bay, three tanks in the rear deck, and one in the radio compartment. Only the radio compartment tank—possibly because of its proximity to so much electrical equipment—was self-sealing; the rest of the tanks were aluminum vessels.

The flight tests were made at Eglin Field beginning 24 April 1943, and ending seven weeks later. Some bugs had to be ironed out: Initially, the B-24 tanker's line-firing gun was elevated so high that the cable was cut by the Liberator's left outboard propeller as the line played out. Realigning the gun to a horizontal position eliminated this problem. The USAAF flew these refueling sorties at about 150 miles an hour—this was faster than the speed used by the British, which, according to the testers, "made it

necessary to increase the angle of the contact gun from 32 and a half degrees to 40 degrees forward to prevent the cable from being broken by the snap load applied" when the cable was expended. They also noted: "The location of the gun caused the contact cable to be blown back by the propeller blast of the tanker, decreasing the distance the cable was thrown toward the bomber." This effect was reduced by shielding the box in which the cable was stored. "After the above-mentioned corrections were made, the making of contact between the tanker and bomber was consistently successful." (Army Air Forces Materiel Engineering Division Memorandum Report on Refueling in Flight, Serial No. ENG-51/B853, Add. 2 [MX-204], 25 June 1943.)

Five contact flights were made in which no gasoline was transferred, to give the crews experience in the equipment's use. It was during these flights that the AAF crews determined that the increase in airspeed over the British use of the system resulted in significantly

increased drag on the cable and hose between the two airplanes. Subsequently, the cable used to pull the hose into the B-17 receiver's coupling was increased from 1,300-pound test strength to 2,000-pound test, while the length of hose was extended to 235 feet. It took the USAAF crews an average of five minutes to make, and break, contact, from the time the contact gun was fired, and the reeling and connecting operations were made, until the airplanes broke contact, not counting the actual fuel transfer time of about 13 minutes for 1,500 gallons. The most difficult part of the operation was making contact. This was eased when the testers applied markings on the cable trailed by the B-17, to permit the tanker pilot to formate in proper position by observing the markings. (In modern day boom refueling operations, the receiver formates on the tanker, using a combination of painted cues on the boom and light signals from the boom operator.) Seven fuel transfer flights were performed; the sixth fuel-transfer sortie was photographed from another aircraft.

For breakaway after refueling, the B-17 crew allowed the hose to trail about 350 feet behind it, attached to the hauling line. According to the June 18, 1943 Flight Section report: "When the hauling (line) is completely out (350 feet) there is a weak link in the line and (the) B-24 simply flies slowly off to the right." The testers also noted in this report: "There is a slight tendency for the B-24D to skid around while the hose is trailing free, but as it is

Line gun in B-24 bomb bay shot steel cable toward trailing line from B-17 to effect refueling contact. (Air Force photo)

wound back into the B-24D this disappears."

The testers concluded that the refueling equipment was practical. "The operation of the equipment leading to the transfer of gasoline, and the operations necessary for breaking contact are straightforward mechanical operations within the ability of the average line mechanic or crew member of either airplane," the 25 June 1943 report concluded. It was recommended that future installations take advantage of tankage modifications in the B-24 intended to permit increased flow rate, thereby diminishing refueling time. This report also recommended that: "Careful consideration be given to the use of this method of refueling in flight for the purpose of extending the present range of B-17 airplanes."

A 20 July 1943 Engineering Division memorandum report included an appendix depicting an operational mission using a B-24D tanker and a B-17F bomber, in which the B-17 would take on 1,400 gallons of gas from the accompanying B-24 1,344 miles from the takeoff point, thereby allowing the B-17 to continue to a target 1,900 miles from takeoff with 6,000 pounds of bombs, spend up to 15 minutes over the target area, and return, all the while using a strict cruise efficiency regimen. (Engineering Division Memorandum Report No. ENG-50-914, 20 July 1943, Appendix V—Sample Flight Plan Employing Flight Refueling [MX-204]).

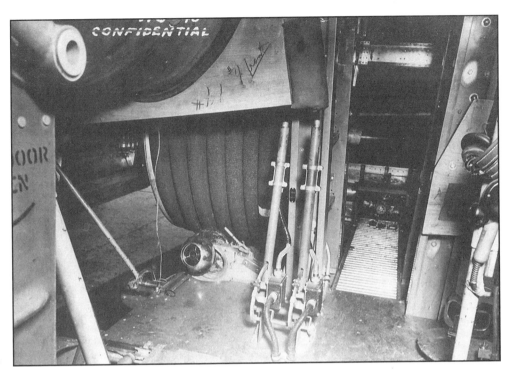

Details of B-24D's refueling hose and nozzle are visible. (Air Force photo)

A subsequent tactical analysis of the refueling operation concluded: "This system is not adaptable to bombardment aircraft due to the fact that excessive modification of each aircraft is necessary. Also the exposed fuel lines in the receiver airplane creates a fire hazard if the aircraft is attacked by the enemy. For bombardment purposes this operation would require two squadrons to do the work of one." The possibility of fighter attack during refueling made the operation vulnerable.

However, the tactical analysis concluded: "The equipment could be used successfully for long range reconnaissance in the Pacific area where interception is unlikely." The tacticians recommended in 1944 that: "The present installations be removed from the airplanes which are restricted from combat, and sent to the 13th Air Force for installation in tactical airplanes. It is believed that one tanker airplane and one receiver airplane is suffi-

cient for that area." The reports on this project do not record if such an operational installation was made. (Army Air Forces Board Project No. [T] 9—Tactical Application and Test of Refueling in Flight of Heavy Bombardment Aircraft, 10 March 1944.)

Availability of longer-ranging B-29s and bases ever closer to Japan diminished the urgency of wartime refueling that had been felt originally in the dark days of 1942 when Japan's net was farthest flung. But the hose, line, and grappling hook method of aerial refueling would be revisited with operational B-29s of Strategic Air Command in 1948, followed soon thereafter by Boeing's more effective flying boom.

Still, the history of aerial refueling must credit a wartime B-24D Liberator with pioneering the tactical utility of this range-extending operation.

VERSATILE FOR VICTORY

The C-87 Liberator Express was a convenient adaptation of the B-24 to transport use ordered by the USAAF in 1942. With more usable volume than a B-17, the Liberator lent itself to cargo transformation on the Consolidated-Vultee Fort Worth, Texas, assembly line, where, initially, B-24Ds were converted to C-87s.

C-87s typically carried 21-25 passengers in airline seats, on a floor that kept all seats essentially on a level plane as the fuselage sloped up toward the tail. High-priority cargo such as aircraft spare parts also were ferried expeditiously by C-87s during the war. The Navy operated C-87 variants under the designations RY-1 and RY-2. At the end of the war, transport designs including the C-54 were available in abundance, and C-87s quickly left the Air Force. At least one example of the transport Liberator Express entered the civilian postwar market, and in the late 1960s, two ex-Royal Air Force Liberator Express aircraft were retained by the Indian Air Force.

In late 1942, Col. E. H. Alexander argued on behalf of arming C-87s for the India-China Wing of the AAF: "I recommend the replacement of unarmed C-87s now assigned this Wing with fully armed aircraft of the same type… In support of General Chennault's proposed offensive, armed C-87s will

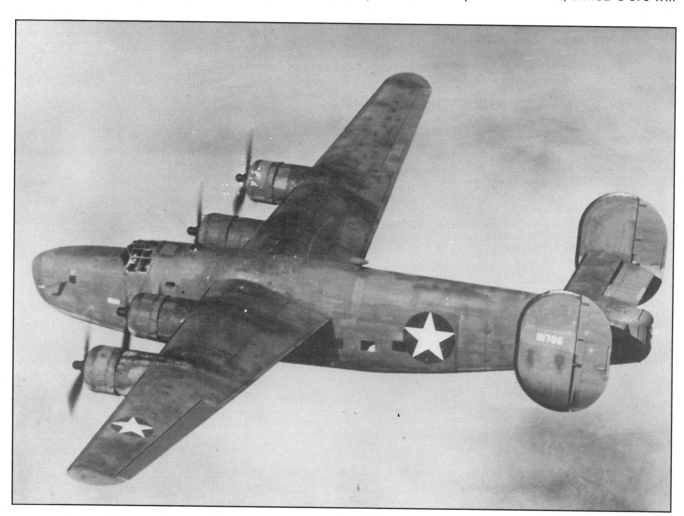

Early C-87 (41-11706) carried a number originally assigned to a B-24D-CO. Blunt early-style tail cap on this C-87 had provision for a single .50-caliber machine gun. (Peter M. Bowers collection)

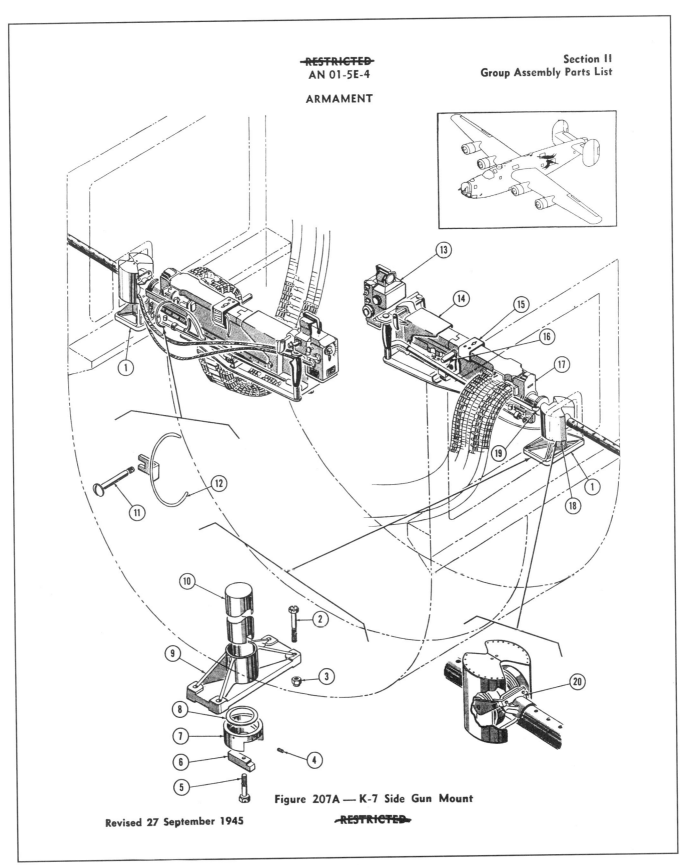

~~RESTRICTED~~

Figure 207A — K-7 Side Gun Mount

When using K-7 waist gun mounts, B-24 manual called for modifications to create azimuth stops [parts 6-10]. K-7 mount was used in concert with E-13 recoil adaptor [part 14] and K-13 compensating gunsight [part 13]. Drawing shows J-4 gun heaters [part 15] clamped to top covers of machine gun receivers. (Courtesy Carl Scholl, Aero Trader)

Seating in the Liberator bombers converted into transports did not always follow C-87 standard, as seen by the double row in the left of the photo. Wing center section is visible at top. (Air Force photo.)

be necessary to lay emergency supplies on advanced tactical airdromes from time to time. I believe that all C-87s in this Wing after next November 1 (end of monsoon season) should be armed with one caliber .50 machine gun in the tail, two fixed caliber .50 guns in the nose, a power driven top turret mounting two guns of the same size, and one flexible belly gun." This was said to be the armament applied to C-87 number 41-11800, Colonel Alexander said. "It is with the C-87s that I expect to deliver supplies

When aging LB-30s were returned to the United States for conversion to transport use, they became virtual C-87s with the addition of windows and seating. A built-up belly structure replaced the bomb bay. (Air Force photo.)

WARBIRD**TECH**
S E R I E S

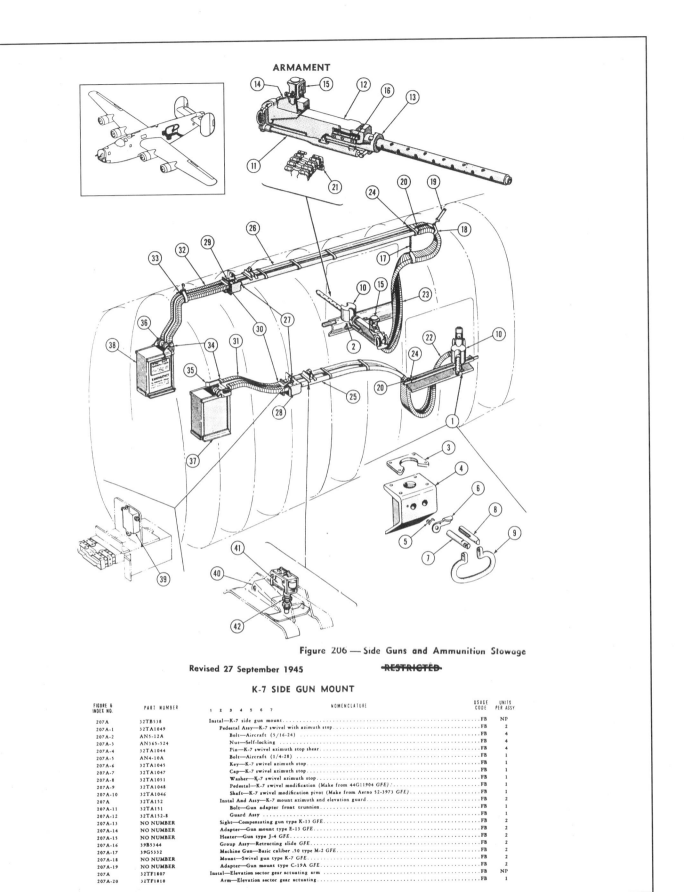

Figure 206 — Side Guns and Ammunition Stowage

Revised 27 September 1945   ~~RESTRICTED~~

K-7 SIDE GUN MOUNT

FIGURE & INDEX NO.	PART NUMBER	1 2 3 4 5 6 7 NOMENCLATURE	USAGE CODE	UNITS PER ASSY
207A	32TB538	Instal—K-7 side gun mount..	FB	NP
207A-1	32TA1049	Pedestal Assy—K-7 swivel with azimuth stop................................	FB	2
207A-2	AN5-12A	Bolt—Aircraft (5/16-24)..	FB	4
207A-3	AN365-524	Nut—Self-locking..	FB	4
207A-4	32TA1044	Pin—K-7 swivel azimuth stop shear...................................	FB	4
207A-5	AN4-10A	Bolt—Aircraft (1/4-28)..	FB	1
207A-6	32TA1045	Key—K-7 swivel azimuth stop.......................................	FB	1
207A-7	32TA1047	Cap—K-7 swivel azimuth stop.......................................	FB	1
207A-8	32TA1051	Washer—K-7 swivel azimuth stop....................................	FB	1
207A-9	32TA1048	Pedestal—K-7 swivel modification (Make from 44G11904 GFE)...............	FB	1
207A-10	32TA1046	Shaft—K-7 swivel modification pivot (Make from Aerno 52-3973 GFE).........	FB	1
207A	32TA152	Instal And Assy—K-7 mount azimuth and elevation guard...................	FB	2
207A-11	32TA151	Bolt—Gun adapter front trunnion....................................	FB	1
207A-12	32TA152-8	Guard Assy..	FB	1
207A-13	NO NUMBER	Sight—Compensating gun type K-13 GFE..............................	FB	2
207A-14	NO NUMBER	Adapter—Gun mount type E-13 GFE..................................	FB	2
207A-15	NO NUMBER	Heater—Gun type J-4 GFE..	FB	2
207A-16	39B5344	Group Assy—Retracting slide GFE....................................	FB	2
207A-17	39G5332	Machine Gun—Basic caliber .50 type M-2 GFE..........................	FB	2
207A-18	NO NUMBER	Mount—Swivel gun type K-7 GFE....................................	FB	2
207A-19	NO NUMBER	Adapter—Gun mount type C-19A GFE..................................	FB	2
207A	32TF1807	Instal—Elevation sector gear actuating arm.............................	FB	NP
207A-20	32TF1810	Arm—Elevation sector gear actuating.................................	FB	1

Overhead ammo tracks and flexible chutes fed waist guns in K-6 mounts. Enclosed B-24 waist windows were directly opposite each other; to afford gunners more room, gun mounts were staggered in the openings.

Heavily-retouched Air Force photo shows XB-41 bomber escort armament, including dual waist guns and second dorsal turret on command deck aft of wing. Unlike similarly-devised XB-40 version of the B-17, the XB-41 did not make any combat trials in Europe.

where active hostile air action may be expected daily."

A letter from Air Transport Command (ATC) headquarters, dated Nov. 27, 1942, reported: "Approval has been obtained to arm the 12 C-87 aircraft scheduled for the India-China Wing." But the ATC letter does not mention tail guns. The first of these C-87s was forecast to leave the United States December 15, 1942.

Whether or not armed C-87s reached India, variations on transport Liberators, including scarcely-made-over B-24 bombers, were employed at times in some overseas locations. The factory provision for a tail gun was lost with the introduction of a streamlined tail cone on most production C-87s.

Air Transport Command (ATC) civilian airline pilots, flying C-87s under contract, were not uniformly enthusiastic about their Liberator Express cargo airplanes in 1943. W.L. Trimble, captain in charge of Trans World Airways (TWA) C-87 operations in Natal, wrote on January 21, 1943, to H.F. Blackburn in Washington, D.C.: "Several weeks ago the TWA boys got together with the PAA (Pan American Airways) gang for a general bull session and to discuss a recent series of accidents involving C-87s and converted Liberators..." Trimble's account said American Airlines (AA) grounded its C-87s to fix problems. The TWA pilot listed the fliers' gripes with their Liberator transports, which he said American Airlines had already fixed on their assigned aircraft. The list included:

• "...Redesign gas tank caps so won't siphon and fill wing with fumes...

• Provide some sort of protection for gas lines under the center section to protect them from cargo being thrown against them in rough air.

• Get that 'God-damned' radio transmitter out of the center section. PAA, the Army, and ourselves have all had flash overs and with the fumes that are always in the center section, we have just been lucky...

Original configuration of XB-41 mounted forward top turret higher than normal, no doubt further aggravating this version's performance problems. Early Bendix chin turret ultimately matured as frontal armament on B-17G. (Air Force photo)

ARMAMENT
M6A GUN MOUNT AND HYDRAULIC TUBING

FIGURE & INDEX NO.	PART NUMBER	1 2 3 4 5 6 7 NOMENCLATURE
208A		M6A Gun Mount and Hydraulic Tubing
208A	32TF1223	Instal—Tail gunner's seat sling...................................
208A-1	32TF1222	Sling—Seat
208A-2	AN46-7	Bolt—Eye (3/8-24 for 3/8 pin)
208A-3	AN365-624	Nut—Self-locking
208A	32TF1221	Piping Diagram—M6A gun mount hydraulic system..................
208A-4	32TF1221-13	Tubing Assy—(Make from 03-105-210 GFE)
208A-5	32TF1221-17	Tubing Assy—(Make from 03-105-207 GFE)
208A-6	32TF1221-6	Tubing Assy
208A-7	32TF1221-7	Tubing Assy
208A-8	32TF1221-15	Tubing Assy—(Make from 03-105-215 GFE)
208A-9	03-105-121	Valve—GFE
208A-10	32TF1221-16	Tubing Assy—(Make from 03-105-209 GFE)
208A-11	32TF1221-12	Tubing Assy—(Make from 03-105-213 GFE)
208A-12	32TF1221-10	Tubing Assy—(Make from 03-105-211 GFE)
208A-13	32TF1221-11	Tubing Assy—(Make from 03-105-208 GFE)
208A-14	32TF1221-9	Tubing Assy
208A-15	32TF1221-8	Tubing Assy
208A-16	03-105-205	Hydraulic Line Assy—GFE...............................
208A-17	03-105-206	Hydraulic Line Assy—GFE...............................
208A-18	03-105-204	Hydraulic Line Assy—GFE...............................
208A-19	03-105-214	Hydraulic Line Assy—GFE...............................
208A	32TA1035-3	Instal—M6A gun mount
208A-20	44D4853	Sight—Flexible gun type N8A GFE.
208A-21	32TA1040R	Tube Brace Assy—M6A gun mount
208A-22	AN365-624	Nut—Self-locking
208A-23	AN4-11A	Bolt—Aircraft (1/4-28) ....
208A-24	AN6-11A	Bolt—Aircraft (3/8-24) ....
208A-25	AN365-428	Nut—Self-locking (10-32)
208A-26	NO NUMBER	Gun Mount—Type M6A GFE
208A-27	39G5332	Machine Gun—Basic caliber .50 type M-2 GFE.
208A-28	AN4-10A	Bolt—Aircraft (1/4-28)
208A-29	AN365-428	Nut—Self-locking
208A-30	32TA1037	Mount Assy—Armor plate..........................
208A-31	32TA1036	Armor plate ....
208A-32	NO NUMBER	Heater—Gun type J4 GFE.
208A-33	41D10358	Solenoid—Gun firing type G9 GFE.
208A-34	32TA1040L	Tube Brace Assy—M6A gun mount
208A-35	AN365-1032	Nut—Self-locking
208A-36	AN3-4A	Bolt—Aircraft (10-32) ....

"See page 327 for effective serial numbers."

Seldom-acknowledged tail armament revision posted in a B-24 parts catalog dated after the end of the war depicts the use of a hydraulic M6A twin-.50-caliber mount in a Plexiglas and pliable-boot enclosure. M6A mount is similar to mount used in Martin B-26 tail gun installations.

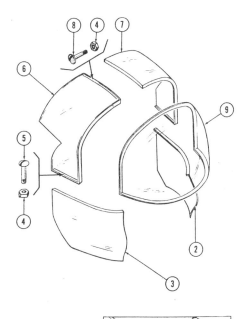

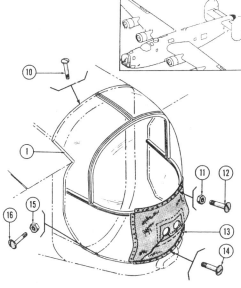

Figure 208B — M6A Gun Mount Enclosure
~~RESTRICTED~~
Revised 27 September 1945

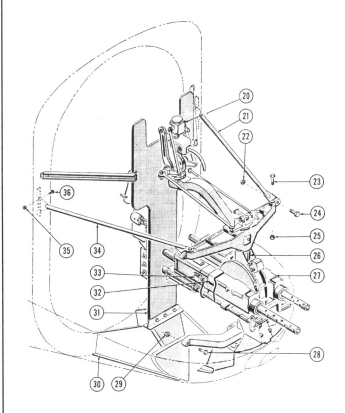

Figure 208A — M6A Gun Mount and Hydraulic Tubing
Revised 27 September 1945

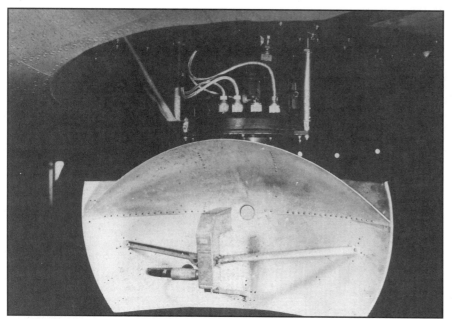

B-24 H2S radar dish for bombing through overcast extended from ball turret opening. A protective radome covered this dish in use. (Air Force photo)

• No oil quantity gauges add zest to the guessing game…

• Take out and throw those black fluorescent (cockpit) lights as far as possible, as they never work and no replacement bulbs available here…

• If you must keep them (fluorescent lights), do as AA (American Airlines) did and put an auxiliary lighting system in so as to get away from the common practice of pilots landing at night by hand-held flashlights. Brother, this isn't funny as the pile of cracked up Libs at Kano (Nigeria) will testify."

Trimble cited problems with the C-87s' retractable landing lights, which he said burned out or got jammed in intermediate positions on occasion. "Since we have no flares and none of these fields have floodlights, it comes under the heading of fun to land these babies at night by moonlight--we don't think." At least part of the problem was one of supply, with landing light lamps scarce. "None of our ships have over one light as no replacements are available and we trade around from one ship to another and from TWA to PAA and vice versa whenever we have a ship due out at night," he explained.

Even while listing complaints about the C-87s, Trimble said his airline compatriots "have just been pretty badly burned up about these ships and all want off them, but they haven't refused to fly them except in one case, but only because it's a military operation and the boys are surprisingly willing to fly long hours, any weather, anywhere with never a gripe."

XB-41 ESCORT LIBERATOR

Before America's entry into World War Two, U.S. Army Air Forces planners mulled the concept of a bomber escort airplane as early as June 1941. Foreign attempts at daylight formation bombing had repeatedly been eviscerated by marauding fighters. At that time, the range of escorting fighters was significantly less than that of the bombers. AAF planners theorized that another bomber, carrying extra ammunition and guns in place of the weight of bombs, could pace the bombers all the way, and spread a protective umbrella of gunfire. By September of 1941, Air Force planners were saying such a

Eagle radar (AN/APQ-7) used a stub wing beneath the fuselage, below the top turret location, to provide a high resolution target image. (Air Force photo)

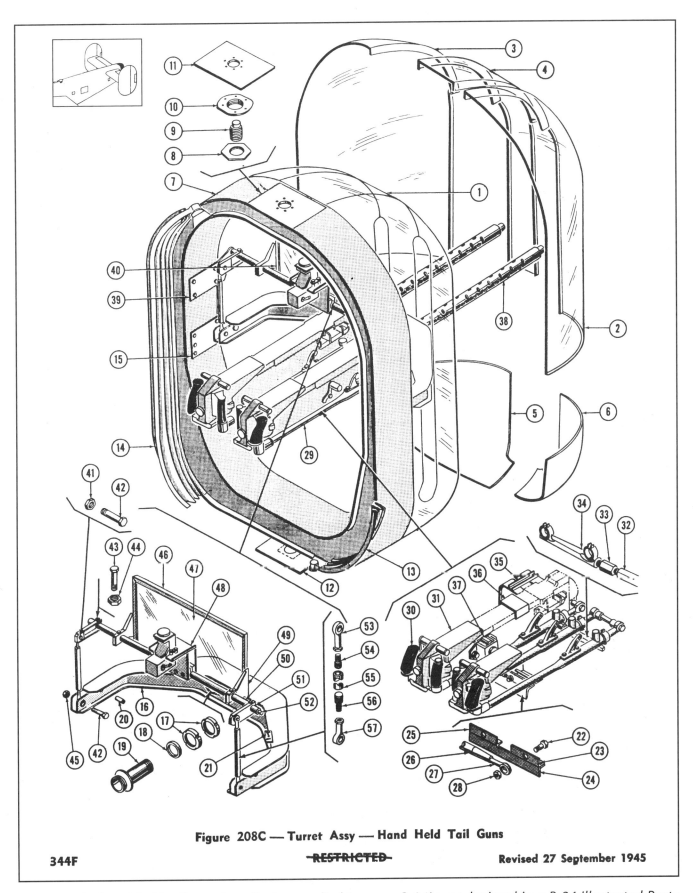

Figure 208C — Turret Assy — Hand Held Tail Guns

RESTRICTED

Revised 27 September 1945

Lightweight hand-held tail gun installation applied to some B-24Ls, as depicted in a B-24 Illustrated Parts Breakdown.

CONSOLIDATED
B-24 LIBERATOR

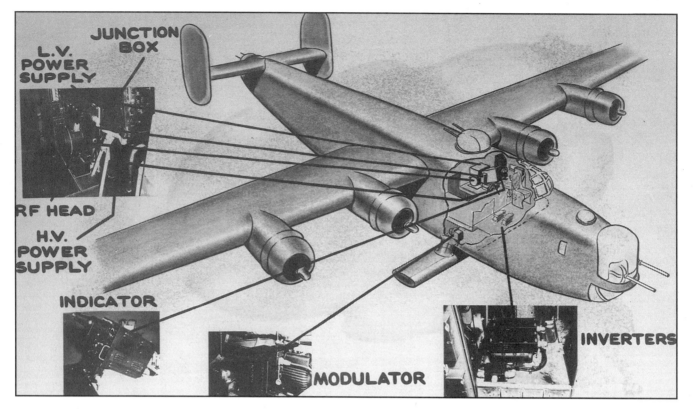

L.V. POWER SUPPLY
JUNCTION BOX
RF HEAD
H.V. POWER SUPPLY
INDICATOR
MODULATOR
INVERTERS

Air Force sketch of Eagle radar installation in a B-24. Eagle saw limited service on B-24s; also on B-29s.

When fledgling B-24 pilots went under a hood for instrument flight training in this Liberator, an enlisted scanner sat in a modified top turret dome to provide a margin of visual safety, circa October 1943. (Air Force photo)

bomber escort should "carry a sufficient number of powerful multi-gunned turrets to match gun fire with any two modern fighters making simultaneous attacks on it," according to an official Air Force document, "Summary of the XB-41 Project." As the bomber-escort concept progressed, planners including Brig. Gen. Muir S. Fairchild emphasized forward defensive fire as the single most important weakness to overcome in B-17s and B-24s. As the bomber escort idea bloomed and rapidly faded, some of the

WARBIRDTECH
SERIES

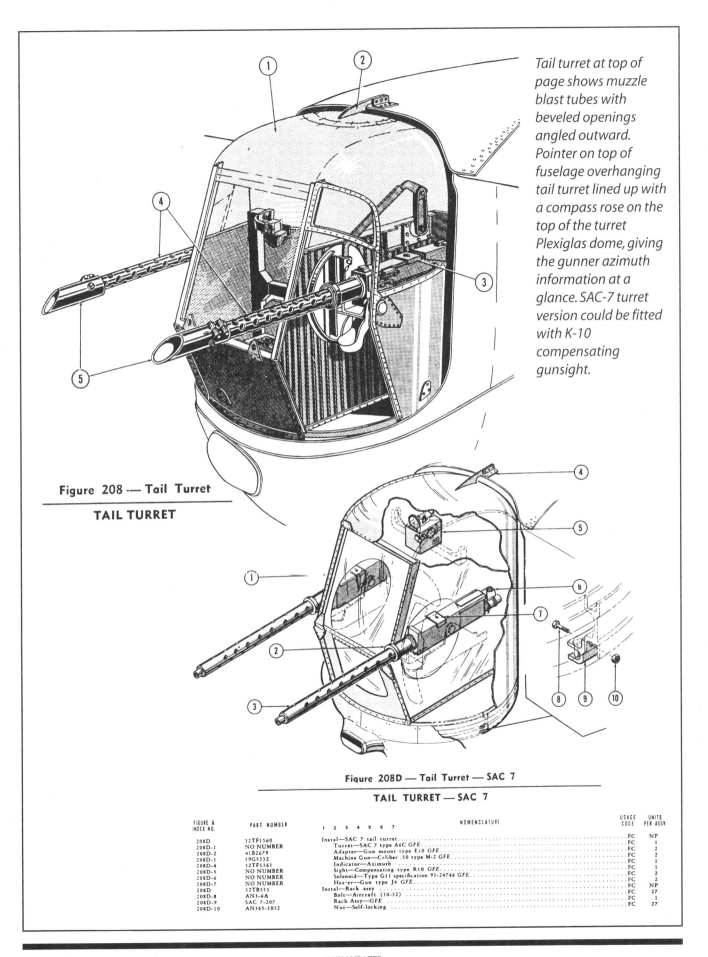

Tail turret at top of page shows muzzle blast tubes with beveled openings angled outward. Pointer on top of fuselage overhanging tail turret lined up with a compass rose on the top of the turret Plexiglas dome, giving the gunner azimuth information at a glance. SAC-7 turret version could be fitted with K-10 compensating gunsight.

Figure 208 — Tail Turret

TAIL TURRET

Figure 208D — Tail Turret — SAC 7

TAIL TURRET — SAC 7

FIGURE & INDEX NO.	PART NUMBER	1 2 3 4 5 6 7 NOMENCLATURE	USAGE CODE	UNITS PER ASSY
208D	32TF1360	Instal—SAC 7 tail turret.	FC	NP
208D-1	NO NUMBER	Turret—SAC 7 type A6C *GFE*.	FC	1
208D-2	41B2679	Adapter—Gun mount type E10 *GFE*.	FC	2
208D-3	39G5332	Machine Gun—Caliber .50 type M-2 *GFE*.	FC	2
208D-4	32TF1361	Indicator—Azimuth	FC	1
208D-5	NO NUMBER	Sight—Compensating type K10 *GFE*.	FC	1
208D-6	NO NUMBER	Solenoid—Type G11 specification 93-24746 *GFE*.	FC	2
208D-7	NO NUMBER	Heater—Gun type J4 *GFE*.	FC	NP
208D	32TB553	Instal—Rack assy	FC	27
208D-8	AN3-6A	Bolt—Aircraft (10-32)	FC	1
208D-9	SAC 7-207	Rack Assy—*GFE*	FC	27
208D-10	AN365-1032	Nut—Self-locking	FC	27

Camera operators on F-7 photo mapping Liberators used for training at Will Rogers Field, Oklahoma, were required to fly 10 missions, take pictures, and be proficient at loading cameras and film magazines in the F-7. Crewman at left holds a film magazine. (Air Force photo)

frontal armament development would linger and resurface in regular bomber variants.

As the bomber escort theory was evolving, the Eighth Air Force in England endorsed the idea in August 1942, calling for completion in a half year to be effective for the operational bomb groups then facing the Luftwaffe. An AAF Technical Report submitted from Europe in August 1942 provided some varied minimum requirements for bomber escort ammunition: Rear guns were to have enough rounds for the equivalent of four minutes of continuous firing; upper and lower turrets should have a two-minute continuous fire equivalency; side guns should carry enough ammunition for one minute of continuous fire, while front guns were to be provisioned for the equivalent of only 30 seconds of continuous firing. (Subsequent tallies of guns and ammunition on the XB-41 showed an allocation of 400 rounds each for the chin turret and two top turrets; 250 rounds each for the waist mounts; 550 rounds for the ball turret, and 800 rounds for the tail turret.)

First into development was an XB-40 escort version of the B-17 Flying Fortress. Near the end of September 1942, the Office of the Director of Military

This San Diego B-24J was configured as an F-7B photo mapping variant, and was used in training at Will Rogers Field, Oklahoma, in a replacement training unit that was part of the Third Tactical Air Division. Oblique camera window is visible to the rear of bomb bay area. (Air Force photo)

FUSELAGE

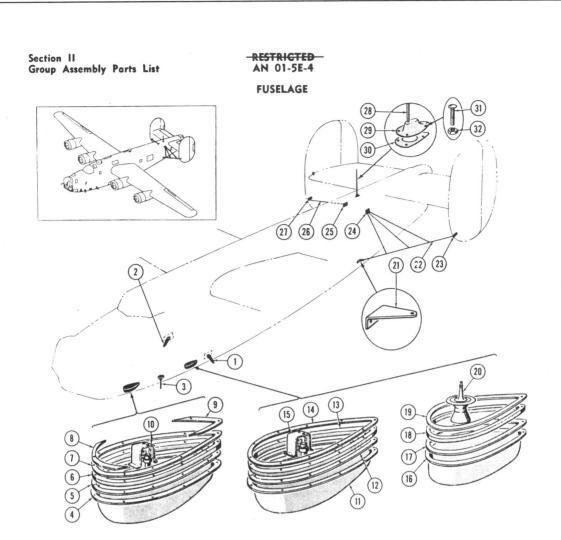

Figure 128A — Radar Counter Measures Antennae

RADAR COUNTER MEASURES EQUIPMENT

FIGURE & INDEX NO.	PART NUMBER	1 2 3 4 5 6 7 NOMENCLATURE	USAGE CODE	UNITS PER ASSY
128B		Radar Counter Measures Equipment (See figure 128A)		
128B	32TF1845	Instal—RCM radio switch box	ANA	NP
128B-1	32TF1924	Mount Assy—RCM radio switch box	ANA	1
128B	32TF1923	Bracket Assy—RCM radio switch box	ANA	1
128B-2	32TF1923-6	Bracket—RCM radio switch box	ANA	1
128B-3	AN8008D2	Insulator—Vibration	ANA	3
128B-4	32TF1848	Box Assy—RCM radio switch	ANA	1
128B-5	AN3202-1	Voltmeter—0-150 volt 400 cycle alternating current	ANA	1
128B-6	AN3022-8	Switch—Three hole mounting single pole toggle	ANA	1
128B-7	M100P	Potentiometer—MAL	ANA	1
128B-8	AN3022-9	Switch—Three hole mounting single pole toggle	ANA	1
128B	32TF1916	Instal—RCM balancing unit	ANA	NP
128B-9	CU63 APT	Balancing Unit—GFE	ANA	1
128B	32TF1692	Instal—RCM inverter and dynamotor	ANA	NP
128B-10	FT398	Mount—Inverter GFE	ANA	1
128B-11	PE218D	Inverter—GFE	ANA	1

"See page 71 for effective serial numbers."

When equipped with radar countermeasures, B-24s were studded with antennas including teardrop blisters on the lower forward fuselage.

B-24 cockpit with style of control wheels and wheel column housings introduced during D-model production. Instrument panel was painted dark green (a close match is federal standard FS 34092). Black box to left of throttles is Honeywell turbosupercharger control; some B-24s used four levers for turbosuperchargers.

Requirements emphasized the parallel need for a Liberator escort variant, issuing a requirement for the quick conversion of six each, B-24s and B-17s, the XB-41 summary history report said.

A D-model B-24 from Eglin Field (41-11822) was sent back to the Consolidated plant at San Diego to become the XB-41. By 12 January 1943, the Director of Military Requirements requested the Materiel Command at Wright Field to convert 13 B-24Ds into service-test YB-41s for use in England. But from the start, the XB-41 showed unimpressive climb rates and ceilings, while exhibiting an unsatisfactory center of gravity. Aside from these detractions, the added armaments (chin turret, second top turret, and doubled waist guns) appeared suitable. Changes were ordered, including the modifications needed to install wide paddle propeller blades, and the use of a newer-type chin turret. The first chin turret contemplated for the Liberator had a different gunsight arrangement than that on the test-bed B-17F, with the B-24 "having a

C-87 42-107263 shows camouflage gray demarcation details. (Al Lloyd collection)

19. FUSELAGE EQUIPMENT. (See figure 370.)

a. PERSONAL EQUIPMENT.

(1) DRINKING WATER. *(See figure 371.)* — A removable two-gallon thermos jug is mounted on a bracket in the forward right-hand corner of main compartment. This jug is fitted with a spigot opening at the base. A paper cup dispenser is also provided at left of jug.

(2) LAVATORY WATER TANK.—Mounted in the tail compartment on the right wall is a reservoir for supplying water for lavatory use.

(3) SUN VISORS AND GLARE CURTAINS. *(See figure 372.)*—Both pilot and copilot are provided with sun visors which are attached separately to arms equipped with ball and socket joints. Glare curtains are also provided for comfort when flying in extremely sunny weather.

(4) COAT RACK AND HOOKS.—A wooden rod attached to the left and right side of fuselage at station 5.2 is provided for hanging clothing. Coat hooks at the lavatory compartment are also provided.

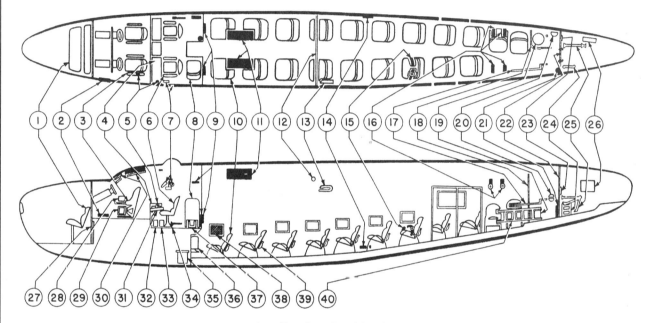

LEGEND

1. Extra Troop Seat*
2. Hand Fire Extinguisher (CCL4 Type)
3. Pilot's and Co-pilot's Seats
4. Navigator's Tables
5. Ash Receptacles
6. Radio Operator's and Navigator's Seats
7. Very Pistol & Pyrotechnic Equipment
8. Commanding Officer's Seat*
9. First Aid Kits

10. Troop Seats
11. Life Rafts
12. Coat Rack
13. Fuel Transfer Hose*
14. Hand Fire Extinguisher (CCL4 Type)
15. Safety Belts (1 Per Seat)
16. Stowage For Two Extra Rafts
17. Hand Starter Crank
18. Lavatory Draw Curtain
19. Toilet
20. Lavatory Basin

21. Portable Fire Extinguisher (CO_2 Type)
22. Tail Compartment Door*
23. Stowage For Summer Plugs*
24. Extra Ladder
25. Tail Jack
26. Water Supply Tank For Lavatory
27. Nose Compartment Door
28. Data Case
29. Flight Report Stowage and Map Case

30. Sun Visors and Glare Curtains
31. Navigators Map Container
32. Night Flying Curtains
33. Blind Flying Curtains*
34. Fire Axe
35. Toilet*
36. Thermos Jug
37. Navigator's Stool*
38. Black Out Curtains
39. Oxygen Mask Stowage
40. Fuel Access Ladder

*Deleted on Later Ships ■ Denotes Emergency Equipment

Figure 370 — Cutaway Showing Location of Fuselage Equipment

A page from the C-87 Erection and Maintenance Manual shows basic C-87 configuration.

Left side of LB-30 Jungle Queen of the 6th Bomb Group was also repeated on other side. Nomenclature block beneath cockpit reads: U.S. Army LB-30, A.C. NO. AL-640. (Ted Small collection)

A Convair employee in Fort Worth watches the entire nose section of a C-87 moving by crane. Faintly visible under chin of C-87 is vestige of a camera port built into some B-24D bombers. C-87 nose hatches are visible to the left of the worker. (Liberator Club)

column rotated in azimuth by the turret, and the B-17F having (the) sight driven both in azimuth and elevation by flexible shafts. The B-17 installation of the gun sight drive proved superior," the XB-41 summary noted. That month, Consolidated said the problem of a too-far-aft center of gravity in the XB-41 could be assisted by putting the Emerson turret in the nose in place of the Bendix chin turret—a switch to be accomplished in the event of a production order for B-41s. Even with the changes requested, on 16 March 1943, the order for 13 YB-41s was canceled, according to the summary.

The modified and upgraded XB-41 returned to Eglin on 28 July 1943. A more satisfactory center of gravity was noted, apparently even without the switch to the Emerson nose turret. (The use of chin turrets in regular bomber B-24s would be revisited several times during the war, as possible solutions to a variety of perceived B-24 deficiencies.) Haunting the XB-41 program now

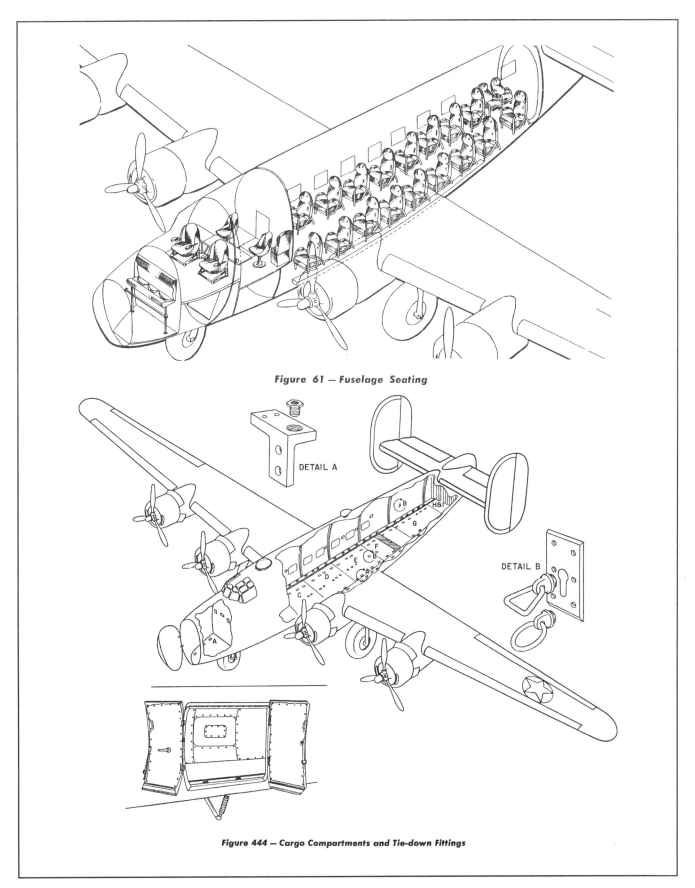

Figure 61 — Fuselage Seating

DETAIL A

DETAIL B

Figure 444 — Cargo Compartments and Tie-down Fittings

Drawings from the Erection and Maintenance manual show how C-87s with seats removed could carry tied-down cargo loaded through large double doors in the left waist position. Right waist window remained as an escape hatch.

Royal Air Force C-87 (Liberator C.VII) carried Pacific markings which deleted red in national insignia, as seen on 18 August 1945 in New Delhi. (Peter M. Bowers)

was the experience of the XB-40 Fortress escort in Europe, which was characterized as "impractical and uneconomical" in the XB-41 summary. The lumbering XB-41 Liberator escort was showing itself to be poor in maneuverability. In some conditions, the XB-41 was 15 miles an hour slower than a regular B-24. Critics said this Liberator escort variant had insufficient addi-tional firepower to justify the absence of a bomb load in a bomber formation. According to the USAAF summary: "On 19 October the Commanding General, Proving Ground Command, told the Deputy Chief of Air Staff that the XB-41 project should be discontin-ued." Two more reports from involved USAAF agencies in November 1943 said the XB-41 pro-ject should be terminated. In December 1943, the Engineering Division found the XB-41 unsuit-able as an escort; on 5 January 1944, the sole XB-41 was taken out of the test world and given to the Central Flying Training Command.

The abortive USAAF excursion into the use of heavy bombers as armed escorts underlined the need for true escort fighters instead of adapted bombers.

U.S. Marine Corps operated some RY-3 transports briefly. RY-3 was C-87 adaptation of Privateer. Aircraft number 4 (probably BuAer No. 90049) was photographed in Peiping, China, in February, 1946. (Liberator Club)

WARBIRD**TECH**
SERIES

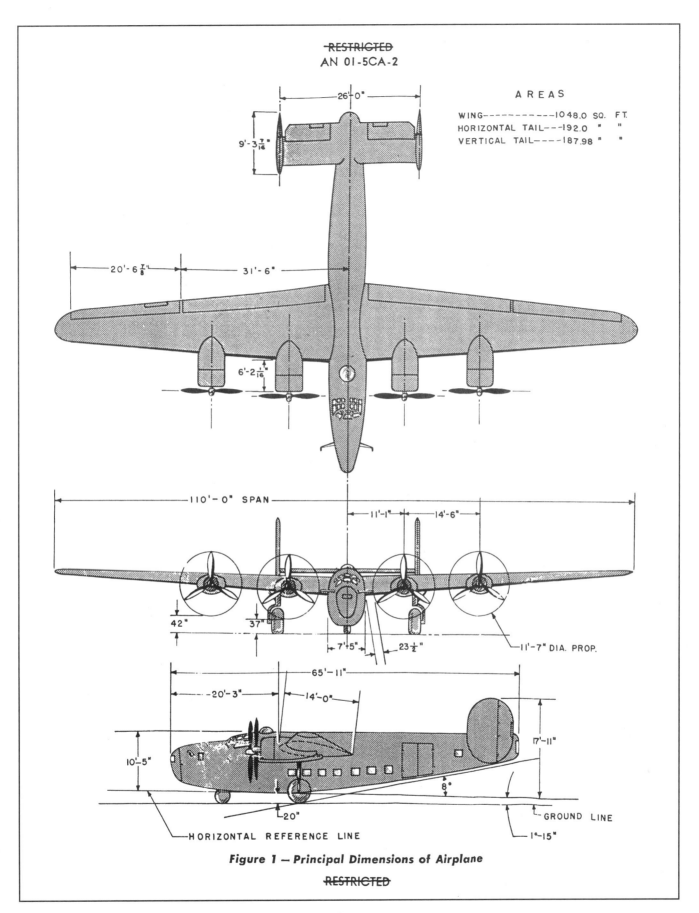

Figure 1 — Principal Dimensions of Airplane

RESTRICTED

Excerpted from C-87 Erection and Maintenance Manual.

CONSOLIDATED
B-24 LIBERATOR

Marine RY-3 BuAer No. 90044. (John Campbell collection)

RADAR MINE-LAYING

Radar-equipped B-24Js and Ls of the 42nd Bomb Squadron, 11th Bomb Group, Seventh Air Force, sowed mines at Chichi Jima and Haha Jima in 1944 in an effort to deny these moorages to the Japanese. In the Bonin Island group, Chichi and Haha Jima were the focus of Project Mike, which mined some harbors in the Bonins. The Liberators of Project Mike carried an SCR-717B search radar, AN/APQ-5 low altitude bombsight (LAB), and SCR-718 radar altimeter for use as high as 40,000 feet—not that such a height was used. The mine-laying Liberators also flew with AN-APN-1 radar altimeter gear, but this equipment's limited altitude range of 4,000 feet made it useless on most of the mining sorties.

The radar equipment imposed a weight penalty that was offset by *(text continued on page 70)*

B-24M 44-42110 at Myitkyina, Burma, 1945. Bomb bay contains gas tank, making this a de facto C-109, although not fully modified as such. (Ken Sumney via SDAM)

COLORFUL CHARACTERS

The Liberator went through several sets of colors in its operational career, embracing camouflages and brilliant natural metal sheen as dictated by mission requirements. To this basic background were applied regulation insignia and markings, often followed by specialized unit codes and personalized names and artwork.

The large number of B-24s built, coupled with the temptingly-flat fuselage sides, meant an abundance of personalized nose art flourished on Liberators.

The B-24J-CF brought from India to the United States by collector David Tallichet flew from the picturesque Bayview, Washington, airport in May 1977 during filming of a television movie about the life of Joe Kennedy, Jr., who was killed in the crash of a PB4Y-1 in England. This B-24J was later bought by Florida collector Kermit Weeks. (Photo by Frederick A. Johnsen)

Bold red and white tail signifies a 466th Bomb Group B-24, based in England with the Eighth Air Force. Billowing parachutes were improvised to slow the bomber when its brakes were lost. (USAF photo)

Variations in typical paint and markings can help identify different B-24 types.

The accompanying photographs amply depict the personality of Liberators and Privateers—as well as the personalities of the men who crewed them.

Many photographers—some official, others earnestly amateur—recorded the life of the Liberator on film.

We are forever indebted to their efforts, for through their images, the B-24 still comes to life as surely as the oil drips from the bottom cylinders of radial engines.

Short-nosed B-24A carries large U.S. flags to proclaim the origin of this Liberator during the period when America was neutral before the bombing of Pearl Harbor. Camouflage pattern is British style. (USAF photo)

Alley Oop carried tail markings for the 465th Bomb Group of the 15th Air Force, serving with the 780th Bomb Squadron. (Tom Foote collection)

WARBIRDTECH
SERIES

Privateer tail attachment details and turret highlights are visible in this 1980 study of a PB4Y-2 stored for many years by Hawkins and Powers Aviation at Greybull, Wyoming. (Photo by Frederick A. Johnsen)

Diamond Lil, *the often-altered LB-30B (assigned RAF number AM927), preserved by the Confederate Air Force, is the oldest Liberator example extant. During the war, Consolidated kept this aircraft as a transport. Subsequent civilian operators registered it as N1503; the CAF registered it as N12905 after returning it from civilian ownership in Mexico. A nationwide campaigner,* Diamond Lil *has been seen by thousands on tours around the United States, as when this photo was taken in July 1987 near Tacoma, Washington. (Photo by Frederick A. Johnsen)*

The last known Ford B-24J in existence was permanently displayed at the Eighth Air Force Museum at Barksdale AFB, Louisiana, along with a tribute to prisoners of war and missing-in-action military members, when photographed in October 1995. (Photo by Frederick A. Johnsen)

Civil-owned B-24J All American (ex-Indian Air Force) touched down at Tacoma, Washington, in 1992 during a tour. (Photo by Frederick A. Johnsen)

Privateer drone BuAer No. 59872 spent its last days at Point Mugu, California. (Jim Morrow collection)

Festooned with colorful paint spots where combat skin patches were made, plus a Mediterranean map depicting its sorties, the 98th Bomb Group's B-24D, nicknamed The Squaw, was sent back to the United States after more than 70 missions, including the dangerous low-level Ploesti raid of August 1, 1943. A morale-building stateside tour awaited The Squaw later that year.

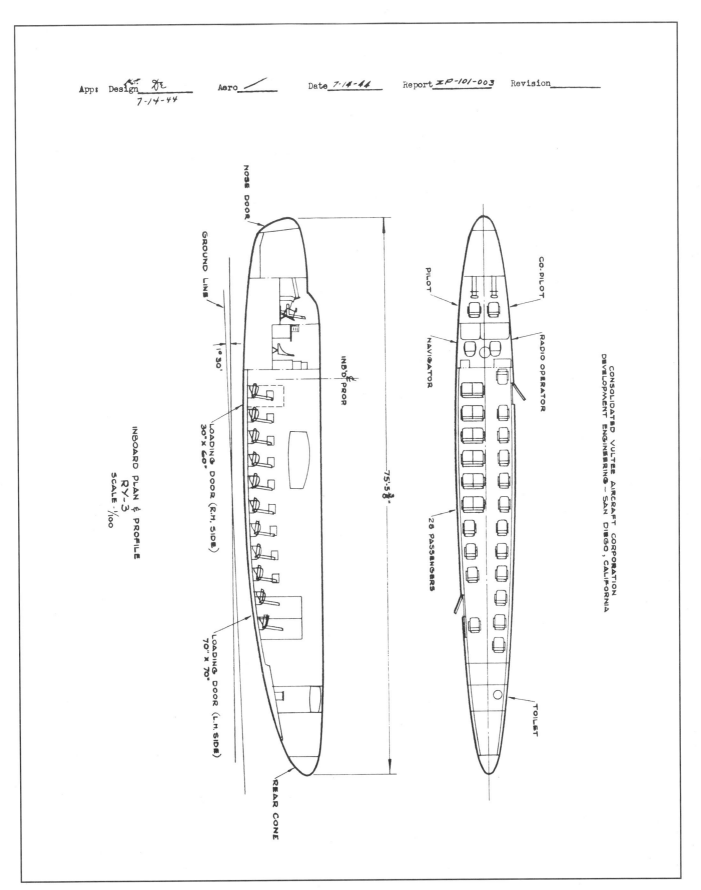

NOSE DOOR

GROUND LINE

1° 30'

INB'D PROP.

LOADING DOOR (R.H. SIDE)
30" x 60"

LOADING DOOR (L.H. SIDE)
70" x 70"

REAR CONE

75'-5⅜"

INBOARD PLAN & PROFILE
RY-3
SCALE -1/100

PILOT

CO-PILOT

NAVIGATOR

RADIO OPERATOR

28 PASSENGERS

TOILET

CONSOLIDATED VULTEE AIRCRAFT CORPORATION
DEVELOPMENT ENGINEERING — SAN DIEGO, CALIFORNIA

RY-3 engineering drawing shows fuselage details including placement of seating, plus new door on right side of fuselage behind cockpit. Privateer length gave room for extra passengers over earlier C-87s. (SDAM)

Unusual spacing of windows suggests this Navy/ Marine RY-style transport Liberator is a post-production field conversion of a bomber variant.

C-109s hauled gasoline onto the European continent to support Allied land operations in the winter of 1944. Operable bomb bay doors typically were retained on C-109s. (Ken Glassburn photo)

(*text continued from page 64*) removing all but the tail guns of Project Mike Liberators, and providing these two weapons with only 200 rounds each—indicative of the diminishing threat posed by Japanese fighters in the region. According to a USAAF Air Proving Ground Command report, ball turrets were also removed from the B-24Js of Project Mike. (Since the report does not mention ball turret removal on the L-models, it is reasonable to deduce these B-24Ls, like many in the Pacific, already flew without ball turrets, using a hand-held ventral mount in place of the full ball.)

All of Project Mike's radar missions carried the one-ton AN Mk-25 aerial mine with a six-foot parachute. On some low-altitude missions, 1,000-pound AN Mk-26-1 mines were used, since these lighter mines could be dropped

C-109 in Europe, circa 1945, with flat window in navigator's compartment, unlike typically-bulged windows in Liberator bomber variants of comparable vintage. (Joseph Obendorff collection)

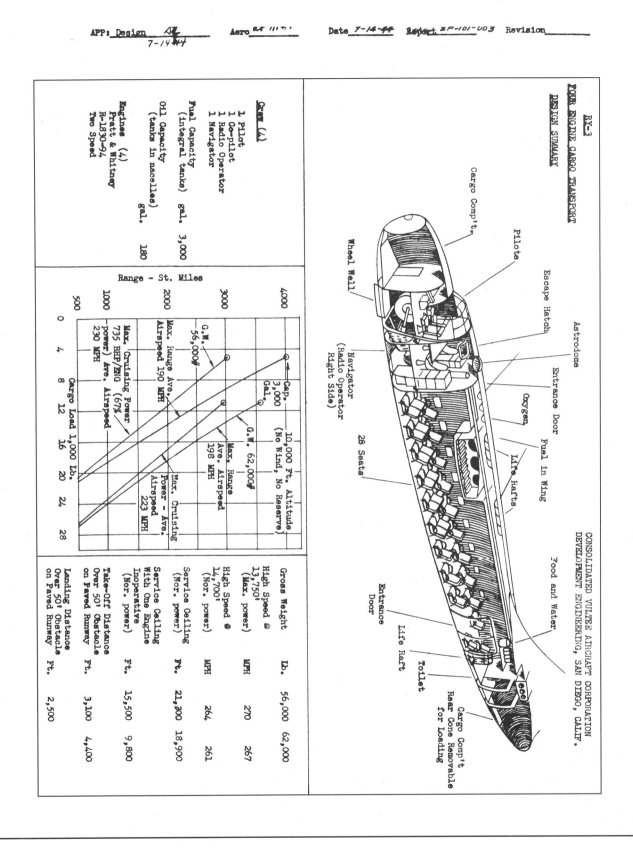

RY-3
FOUR ENGINE CARGO TRANSPORT
DESIGN SUMMARY

CONSOLIDATED VULTEE AIRCRAFT CORPORATION
DEVELOPMENT ENGINEERING, SAN DIEGO, CALIF.

Labels on drawing: Cargo Comp't., Pilots, Escape Hatch, Astrodome, Wheel Well, Entrance Door, Oxygen, Navigator (Radio Operator Right Side), Fuel in Wing, Life Rafts, 28 Seats, Food and Water, Entrance Door, Life Raft, Toilet, Cargo Comp't Rear Cone Removable for Loading

Crew (4)
1 Pilot
1 Co-pilot
1 Radio Operator
1 Navigator

Fuel Capacity
(integral tanks) gal. 3,000

Oil Capacity
(tanks in nacelles)
gal. 180

Engines (4)
Pratt & Whitney
R-1830-94
Two Speed

Range - St. Miles

Graph values: 4000, 3000, 2000, 1000, 500, 0
G.W. 56,000#
Cap. 3,000 Gal.
G.W. 62,000#
Max. Range Ave. Airspeed 190 MPH
Max. Range Ave. Airspeed 198 MPH
Max. Cruising Power (67% power) Ave. Airspeed 230 MPH
Max. Cruising Power - Ave. Airspeed 223 MPH
735 BHP/ENG
10,000 Ft. Altitude (No Wind, No Reserve)

Cargo Load 1,000 Lb.: 0, 4, 8, 12, 16, 20, 24, 28

		Nor. power	Max. power
Gross Weight	Lb.	56,000	62,000
High Speed @ 13,750' (Max. power)	MPH	270	267
High Speed @ 14,700' (Nor. power)	MPH	264	261
Service Ceiling (Nor. power)	Ft.	21,200	18,900
Service Ceiling With One Engine Inoperative (Nor. power)	Ft.	15,500	9,800
Take-Off Distance Over 50' Obstacle on Paved Runway	Ft.	3,100	4,400
Landing Distance Over 50' Obstacle on Paved Runway	Ft.	2,500	

Convair development engineering drawing and specifications for the RY-3 dated 14 July 1944 depicted the aircraft's interior; crew of four was called for. (SDAM)

C-109 My Lady *shows typical Ford anti-glare panel with notch that follows skin panel line.*

from altitudes as low as 200 feet above the waves. Navy trajectory tables furnished the AAF crews slant range release data for use with the radar bombsight. Night missions used radar pathfinders to illuminate the target with flares to enable visual mine-sowing runs by other aircraft. Radar-equipped Liberators also drew the task of laying mines in heavily defended areas by night. In case of daylight overcast, the radar-equipped B-24s were used, versus non-radar bombers.

TRAINED AT TONOPAH

The high desert of central Nevada is sparsely populated, with few residents to be endangered by, or complain about, warplane operations. Into this splendid isolation, the Tonopah Army Airfield (TAAF) was built at an elevation of nearly 6,000 feet. Opening in July 1942, TAAF initially provided bombing ranges for aircraft from Muroc and March Army Airfields in California. Following the basing of P-39 Airacobra fighters at Tonopah in 1943, B-24 and B-25 units came to Tonopah before heading overseas.

C-109s also served in the China-Burma-India Theater of Operations. (Victor D. Seely collection)

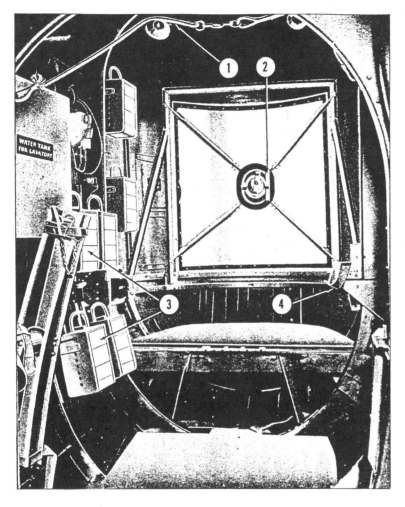

1. Gun Suspension Cord
2. Gun Mount
3. Ammunition Boxes
4. Gun Stowage

Figure 443 — Machine Gun Provisions in Tail Compartment (Early Airplanes)

25. GUNNERY EQUIPMENT.

On the first 42 C-87 airplanes provision was made for the mounting of one .50 caliber machine gun in the tail of the fuselage. A flexible mount and bungee cord was provided for ready mounting of the gun. When not in use the gun was stowed on the left fuselage wall, just forward of the tail window. Six ammunition boxes were mounted on the right fuselage wall opposite the gun stowage. A removable port in the tail window was provided to permit firing the gun when the window was closed. Each window in the troop, or main compartment, is equipped with a port intended to permit defensive fire by troops with rifles or sub-machine guns. All ports are closed by a readily removable Plexiglas stopper. On airplanes after the forty-second, the provision for tail gun installations was eliminated.

Excerpt from C-87 Erection and Maintenance Manual depicts early blunt tail cap with socket for single .50-caliber machine gun.

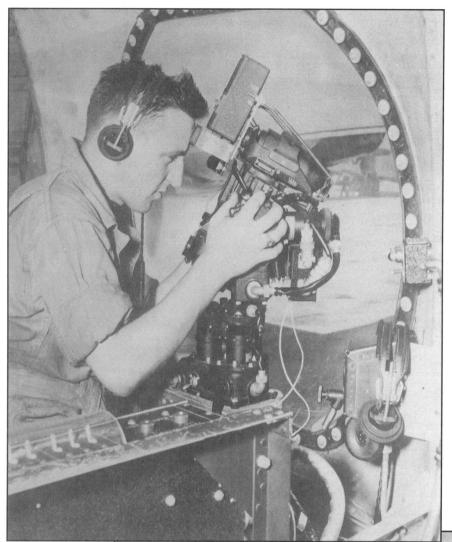

An airman manipulates a B-29 Superfortress remote gunsight in the modified right waist of a TB-24 gunnery trainer at Ft. Myers, Florida, in August 1944. Liberators fitted with B-29 turrets helped train Superfortress gunners at a time when there were more available B-24 airframes than B-29s for stateside use. (Air Force photo)

From 1 February 1944 until the end of the war, Tonopah Army Airfield, in keeping with USAAF training needs, altered the way in which B-24 crews were handled. No longer did a complete bomb group train at Tonopah and depart as a unit. Beginning in 1944, TAAF was a replacement training base, with individual crews coalescing before being sent to existing units overseas as needed. Between 1 February 1944 and 1 August 1945, 742 B-24 combat crews completed their overseas training at Tonopah, according to a neighboring Goldfield, Nevada, newspaper story printed in September 1945.

Bench line-up of late-style E-13 recoil adaptors for enclosed B-24 waist guns, using K-7 mounts and K-13 compensating gunsights. Photo taken at Tonopah AAF, Nevada, on 3 March 1945. (Central Nevada Historical Society, Harvey Herr collection)

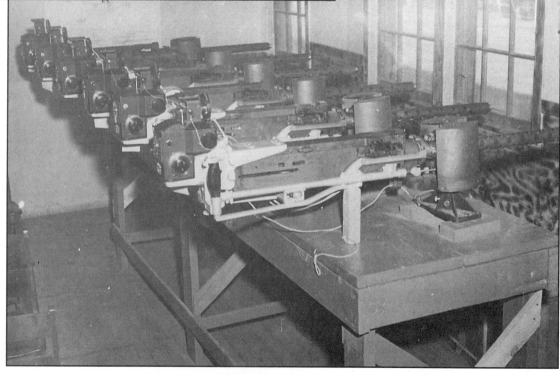

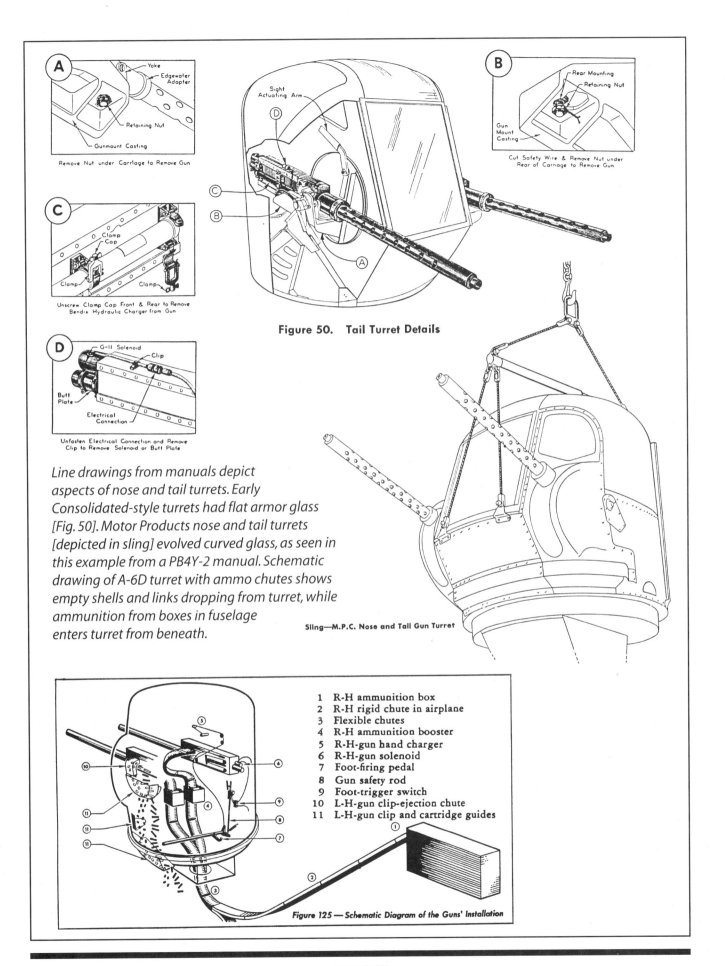

A
Yoke
Edgewater Adapter
Retaining Nut
Gunmount Casting
Remove Nut under Carriage to Remove Gun

B
Rear Mounting
Retaining Nut
Gun Mount Casting
Cut Safety Wire & Remove Nut under Rear of Carriage to Remove Gun

C
Clamp Cap
Clamp
Clamp
Unscrew Clamp Cap Front & Rear to Remove Bendix Hydraulic Charger from Gun

D
G-11 Solenoid
Clip
Butt Plate
Electrical Connection
Unfasten Electrical Connection and Remove Clip to Remove Solenoid or Butt Plate

Sight Actuating Arm
D
C
B
A

Figure 50.   Tail Turret Details

Line drawings from manuals depict aspects of nose and tail turrets. Early Consolidated-style turrets had flat armor glass [Fig. 50]. Motor Products nose and tail turrets [depicted in sling] evolved curved glass, as seen in this example from a PB4Y-2 manual. Schematic drawing of A-6D turret with ammo chutes shows empty shells and links dropping from turret, while ammunition from boxes in fuselage enters turret from beneath.

Sling—M.P.C. Nose and Tail Gun Turret

1 R-H ammunition box
2 R-H rigid chute in airplane
3 Flexible chutes
4 R-H ammunition booster
5 R-H-gun hand charger
6 R-H-gun solenoid
7 Foot-firing pedal
8 Gun safety rod
9 Foot-trigger switch
10 L-H-gun clip-ejection chute
11 L-H-gun clip and cartridge guides

Figure 125 — Schematic Diagram of the Guns' Installation

(382 BGX4 G 12X 34)
SPERRY BALL-TRACKING-PIT-BOTTOM-VIEW

At Tonopah Army Airfield, a stout timber platform mounted a B-24 A-6 tail turret, A-15 nose turret, K-7 waist gun, and a suspended Briggs (Sperry) ball turret, with a Martin upper turret on a dolly beneath the rig. Motion-picture projectors presented gunners with images to track, in a custom-built version of the Air Force's Jam Handy gunnery trainer. (Central Nevada Historical Society, Harvey Herr collection)

TAAF embraced more than 5,175 square miles of desert. The rigors of wartime training saw that landscape dotted with the scars and pyres of crashed Liberators. Some Tonopah veterans ascribed a marked improvement in the base's safety record to the arrival of Col. John A. Feagin as commanding officer in early December 1944.

Before Colonel Feagin's tenure, a string of Tonopah B-24 crashes included the 8 September 1944 night crash of a Liberator carrying tail gunner Caius "Kay" Carpenter. Two other B-24s had already aborted that evening as Kay Carpenter's crew tried a third Tonopah Liberator.

An engine fire blossomed on the third bomber, as the pilots cranked the aircraft back toward the runway. While still about three miles northeast of the field, the stricken B-24 made contact with the gritty desert floor in a wrenching slide through sparse vegetation.

Back at the field, a witness to the drama saw the Liberator's landing lights switch off just before the

Six suspended ball turrets gave new gunners tracking practice at Muroc Army Air Base, circa 1944. (Air Force photo)

Emerson Electric A-15 nose turret details from manual. Only early Emerson domes had full-length front Plexiglas panel; most used an aluminum panel at the bottom.

e. Gunner's Floor Assembly (*Fig. 9*)

The tub-shaped structure that is bolted to the underside of the turntable is known as the Gunner's Floor Assembly. It supports the gunner's seat and affords a mounting frame for the Bumper Stop. There is a large hole in the floor through which ammunition chutes and power cables are brought into turret.

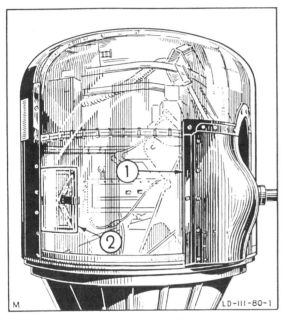

Fig. 8—Dome Assembly

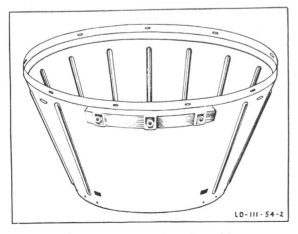

Fig. 9—Gunner's Floor Assembly

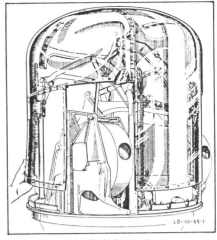

Fig. 56—Method of Removing Dome

Now grasp rear of Dome (**see Fig. 56**) and gently stretch it, while lifting this end clear of obstructions. When rear is clear, a second man should raise front part an equal amount. Jockey Dome carefully to keep it from hitting any part of turret . . . and lift it clear of turret.

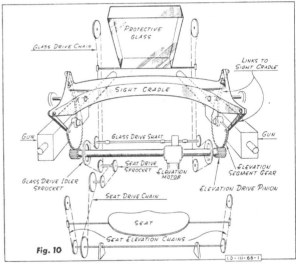

Fig. 10

Elevation Movements (*Fig. 10*)

The guns, sight, seat, control column and bullet-resisting glass (all the "movable units") are elevated or depressed by operation of the Elevation Drive Motor (see schematic illustration of drive). Motor is connected to these various units through a horizontally mounted gear reduction and drive unit (the Elevation Gear Drive Assembly), from the bottom right center of which it is suspended.

The housing of the horizontal drive unit spans the area between the two inboard support assemblies . . . is mounted in each by means of an eccentric, flanged collar (the Torque Tube Eccentrics) which permits adjustment for alignment of the assembly.

A USAAF LB-30 with nose gear trouble, AL573 shows open-air tail gun position and fixed waist window slipstream deflector. Midship Martin dorsal turret was installed on repossessed USAAF LB-30s; Royal Air Force counterparts were designed for Boulton-Paul top turrets with four .303-caliber machine guns. (B.T. Stout collection)

crash. This suggests the copilot, new as he was, nonetheless had presence of mind to strike the B-24's crash bar, cutting off all electrical power to diminish the chance of fire. That last act of the doomed copilot may have saved Carpenter's life, for Kay was hopelessly entangled in the wreckage of the waist section as the Liberator came apart on its slide across the desert.

The blackness of the desert night cloaked the shredded B-24. Rescuers only found the bomber about four hours after the crash, guided by an airman in a commandeered jeep who homed in on the strong fumes of high-octane aviation gasoline leaking from the wreck.

Suffering a broken back and head wounds, Kay Carpenter could only wait as the rescue crew gingerly worked to free him from the mangled aluminum. Later he was told a military policeman, with pistol drawn, had stood outside Kay's line of vision, ready to shoot the trapped gunner as an act of mercy, in case the rescue efforts had ignited the gasoline-soaked wreckage.

Kay Carpenter survived his crash, convalescing in the TAAF hospital.

Another Tonopah alumnus, B-24 co-pilot Dick Cruickshank, reminisced at a 1993 TAAF reunion about the buzz jobs his crew flew over the Nevada desert. Rocketing along at 250 miles an hour, the B-24

On some B-24s, the ball turret was replaced with this lightweight hand-held twin-.50-cal. unit in a shallow Plexiglas dish. (Central Nevada Historical Society, Harvey Herr collection)

WARBIRDTECH
SERIES

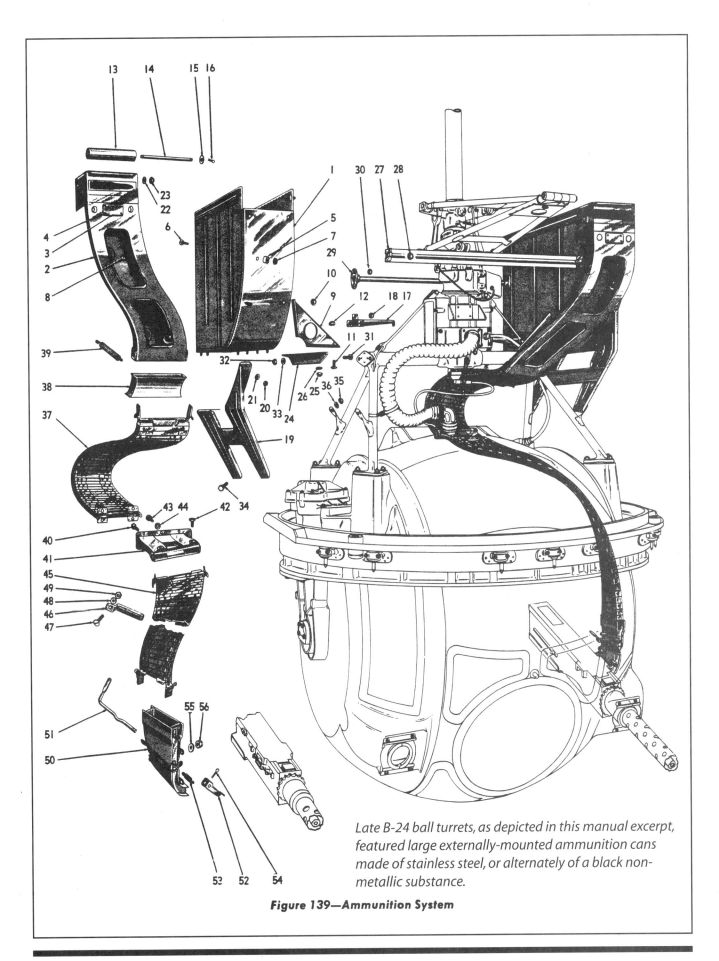

Late B-24 ball turrets, as depicted in this manual excerpt, featured large externally-mounted ammunition cans made of stainless steel, or alternately of a black non-metallic substance.

Figure 139—Ammunition System

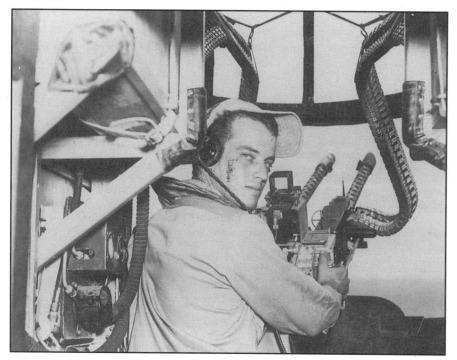

Interior of 5th Bomb Group flexible mount tail gun position shows a pair of E-11 recoil adaptors to carry twin .50-cal. guns. (Edward I. Harrington collection)

pilots relied on the ball turret gunner, suspended beneath the aircraft and calling out altitude adjustments at about 10 feet off the desert's surface, Cruickshank recalled.

More than 100 Tonopah B-24 airmen died in crashes around the isolated air base. Thousands of others survived the Tonopah education, and went on to fly Liberators in combat. If Tonopah had an unusual spate of accidents, it nonetheless represents many B-24 training fields, where young men came together to form unified teams, flying B-24 Liberators.

WALLA WALLA WARRIORS

Fourth Air Force operated several B-24 training bases, including Tonopah, Nevada; Muroc, California; and Walla Walla, Washington. After withdrawal of B-17s from Walla Walla by Second Air Force late in 1943, Fourth Air Force brought B-24s to this pastoral southeastern Washington farm community in April, 1944.

Walla Walla Army Air Field's colorful commanding officer, Col. David Wade, took a proactive, and sometimes mischievous, interest in his Liberator base. After Navy fliers from nearby Pasco, Washington,

Flexible tail gun mount with Plexiglas fairing is evident in this 5th Bomb Group B-24D Patches that survived a mid-air with an out-of-control Japanese fighter. (Cliff Decker collection)

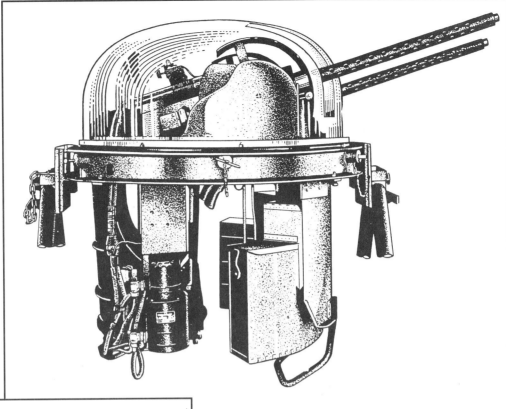

Figure 1 — Complete Turret

RESTRICTED

Martin upper turret with old style dome. Guns could be mounted and removed by elevating 60 degrees above horizontal. Gunner's seat used a drop bottom to permit entry and exit; latches held the seat in place.

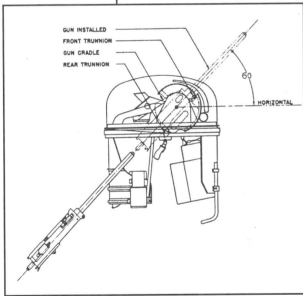

Figure 44 — Installation of Guns

bombed the USAAF base with rolls of toilet paper during a flag ceremony at Walla Walla, Colonel Wade plotted his revenge, according to wartime Walla Walla civic booster Al McVay. In 1976, McVay recalled what happened the day after the Navy raid: About 18 B-24s from Walla Walla, their bomb bays stuffed with garbage and throwaways, roared over the Pasco Navy station, disgorging their contents.

When rumors of supposed B-24 unreliability began dogging the Walla Walla base, Colonel Wade arranged a press flight for Walla Walla newspaper reporter Claude Gray. Gray was toured around southeast Washington and into northeast Oregon, he related years

Employees at the Northwest Airlines modification center in St. Paul, Minnesota, used boresighting tools to align the .50-caliber M-2 machine guns in a B-24 ball turret. A special pit below ground allowed the low-slung ball to be extended with room for the workers. Circular gunner's window consists of two disks of safety glass with an air space between; it is not armor glass. Button at top of circular window is cutout switch which engages a baffle plate designed to interrupt firing of the guns when they could endanger parts of the B-24 including propeller arcs. Empty shells and links drop from chutes beneath guns when firing; this could pose a hazard to other Liberators in tight formations. (Northwest Airlines photo via Steve Mills collection)

Interior of test B-24 Lil' Texas Filley shows B-17 bombardier's seat and chin turret controls. (Air Force photo)

later. Near Boardman, Oregon, the pilot pushed the big desert-sand colored Liberator into a dive, roaring across the landscape at minimal altitude. From a vantage point in the waist of the B-24D, Gray said he could see transmission lines whip past the Liberator as they flew beneath the power lines before resuming a more conservative posture. Gray's pilots had their own points to make about B-24 reliability that day.

Walla Walla Army

Airfield did sustain its share of B-24 accidents. Some may have been the result of using aged B-24s for training with inexperienced crews—a potentially volatile mix. But the punctuations of B-24 mishaps should not detract from the big picture: Walla Walla contributed many Liberator crews to the Air Force in 1944 and 1945.

As B-24s evolved during the war, armaments were adapted and employed to meet enemy threats. Far more than a machine gun was involved—recoil adaptors, gun sights, and related hardware all performed roles in enabling the B-24 to fight back. Some of the Liberator's armament features were:

MUZZLE COMPENSATORS

Muzzle compensators were steel tubes with angled openings, which, when fitted to B-24 tail turrets in a

GUN MOUNT ADAPTOR MARK 6 MOD 3

Parts of the Mark 6 Mod 3

1 FRONT MOUNTING BOLT
2 PISTON RODS AND EYELETS
3 SPACERS
4 WASHER, NUT AND COTTER PIN
5 HYDRAULIC SHOCK ABSORBER UNITS
6 FILLER PLUGS
7 FRONT FRAME SEPARATORS
8 FRONT FRAME SEPARATOR BOLTS
9 BEARER BARS
10 YOKE FITTINGS
11 REAR MOUNTING BOLT
12 REAR MOUNTING SLIDES
13 REAR MOUNTING BRACKET
14 NUT AND COTTER PIN
15 SPADE GRIPS
16 KNURLED SCREWS
17 SIGHT MOUNTING HOLES
18 SIGHT MOUNTING BRACKET
19 BACK GUARD ASSEMBLY
20 TRIGGER
21 SAFETY
22 TRIGGER BAR
23 TRIGGER BAR SPACER AND SPRING

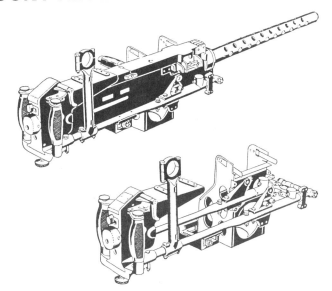

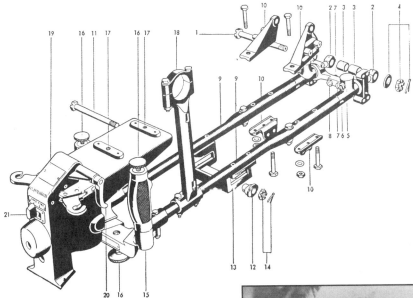

U.S. Navy Mark 6 recoil adaptor as used on waist mounts of some PB4Y-1 Liberators. Mount is basically a single-trigger variant of USAAF E-11 recoil adaptor, with upright bracket for mounting Navy Mark 9 gunsight. (Photo courtesy Ed Darrow)

Some early blocks of Ford B-24Es used this unique greenhouse with gun socket and outside air thermometer protruding in traditional bomb-aiming window. Revised bomb window can be seen beneath this, in slightly altered lower nose contours. (Ray Markman collection)

particular rotation, enhanced accuracy by minimizing vibration. On Consolidated tail turrets in aircraft from 41-23640 and onward, as well as on all tail turrets on earlier B-24s after they had been reworked with gun carriage stiffening and the addition of adjustable sliding mounts, the use of muzzle compensators was prescribed. The gunner's lefthand gun muzzle compensator was to be mounted with the opening facing outboard 35 degrees from horizontal, with the extended beveled lip on the lower side, and the righthand gun muzzle compen-

With its Plexiglas dome removed, this Emerson A-15 nose turret served as a classroom training aid for B-24 (F-7) ground school at Will Rogers Field, Oklahoma, when the photo was taken 29 December 1944. In the photo, frontal slab of armor glass evidently has been disengaged from gun elevation chain drive; typically, the armor glass moved with the guns in elevation, keeping some protection between the gunner and his intended target. (Air Force photo)

sator was to be 55 degrees from horizontal, with the opening facing outboard, to realize the minimum gun vibration and provide the most effective pattern of fire, according to the Erection and Maintenance manual. Early B-24 Consolidated tail turrets featured staggered guns, with the gunner's left weapon protruding further aft than the right gun.

CHEEK GUN SWIVELS

When flexibly-mounted .50-caliber cheek guns were added to the sides of the nose compartments of B-24Ds to provide more frontal firepower, the guns protruded through K-4 spherical ball socket gun mounts which accommodated C-19 adaptors for Bell-designed E-11 recoil adaptors. Photographic evidence shows this to be far and away the predominant cheek gun mount for greenhouse Liberators. And yet several photos of B-24Ds, notably later in the service life of the Liberator, reveal the use of K-5 gun mounts—the same type used in the protruding cheek windows of B-17G Flying Fortresses. The K-5 was a cylindrical mount, with an inner cylinder at 90 degrees to the outer one forming the tube for the gun barrel jacket to rest in. This allowed the outer cylinder to rotate up and down for elevation of the gun, while the inner cylinder could swivel from side to side for azimuth. All of this was baffled to keep wind blast entering the airplane to a minimum.

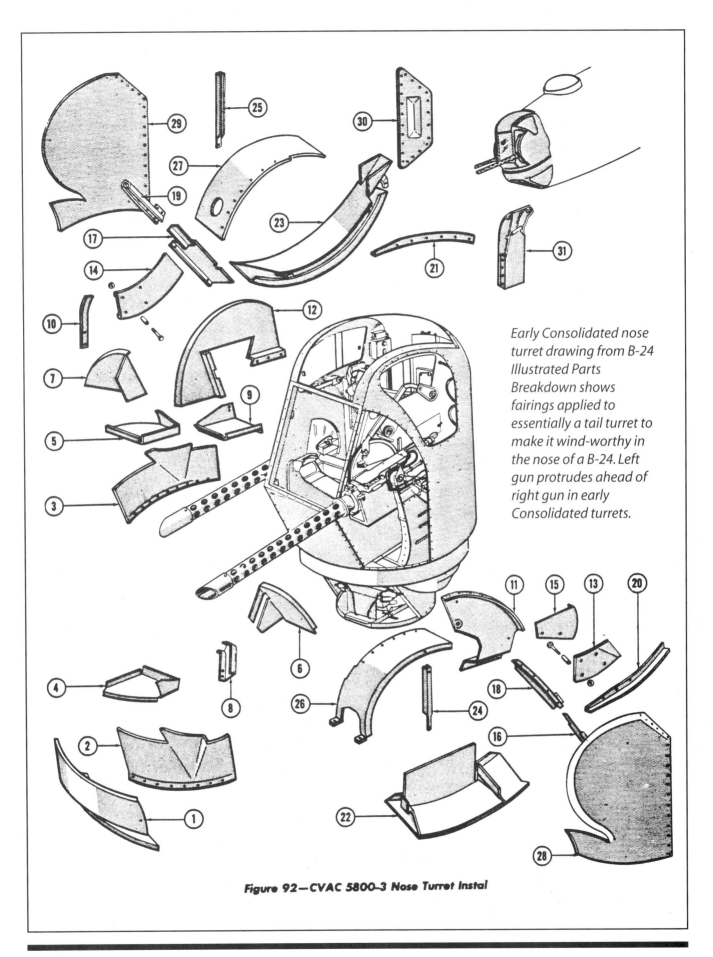

Early Consolidated nose turret drawing from B-24 Illustrated Parts Breakdown shows fairings applied to essentially a tail turret to make it wind-worthy in the nose of a B-24. Left gun protrudes ahead of right gun in early Consolidated turrets.

Figure 92—CVAC 5800-3 Nose Turret Instal

OVER THE BOUNDING MAIN

The U.S. Navy secured a portion of B-24 Liberator production, in addition to acquiring some antisubmarine-warfare B-24Ds from the USAAF. Navy Liberators were designated PB4Y-1 Liberator; the production single-tail development for the Navy was called the PB4Y-2 Privateer.

Fundamental differences attended Naval use of Liberators, compared with most USAAF B-24 bombing missions. Navy PB4Y-1s typically flew solitary sector patrols, sometimes with no predetermined target. Low-level attacks on shipping encountered during such patrols accounted for much of the action seen by PB4Y-1 crews.

VPB-115 TOURED THE PACIFIC

Among Navy Liberator squadrons sent into Pacific combat was patrol bombing squadron VPB-115, flying patrols from January to November 1944. Years after VPB-115's wartime exploits, World War Two veterans of the squadron transcribed official Navy historical reports to disseminate the lore of this aggressive outfit.

From the official record, VPB-115 used 11,125.6 sortie hours to fly 948 sorties after deploying to Munda, New Georgia, in late March 1944. Of these sorties, the largest single group (348 sorties) had a radius of 800 nautical miles; the second largest batch of sorties was 223 that were of 1,000 nautical miles in radius. Twenty-five sorties, most of which were launched from Morotai, had a radius of 1,100 nautical miles.[1]

During the squadron's sorties, a tally of 298 enemy aircraft sightings of all types was compiled, ranging from 35 sightings of twin-engine Betty bombers, to encounters with various Japanese fighters, and 143 unidentified, but listed as enemy, aircraft. These aircraft sightings produced 97 engagements, with some of the Liberator crews aggressively attacking Japanese aircraft.

Eighteen enemy aircraft were destroyed in the air by the gunners of VPB-115, representing the following types:

Early PB4Y-2 Privateer instrument panel carried Consolidated Vultee nameplate for Liberator.

Later production PB4Y-2 instrument panel (right) shows changes in shape and layout from early version. Privateer instrument panels differed from B-24 panels. However, glare shield above center of panel also appears on some late-model B-24s (Ls or Ms) used by the Royal Canadian Air Force, suggesting a common evolution in some cockpit furnishings. (Todd Hackbarth collection)

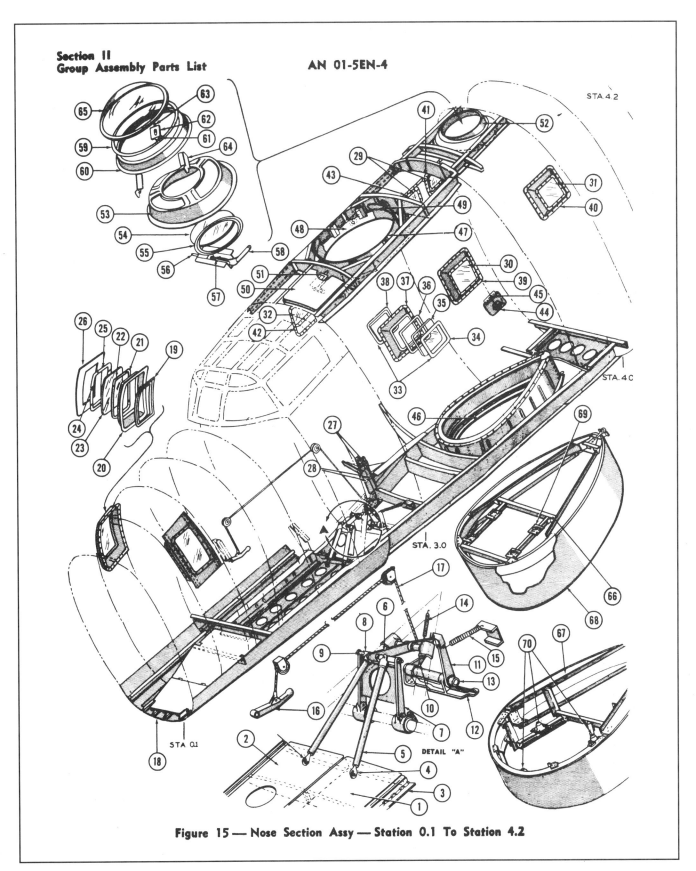

Figure 15 — Nose Section Assy — Station 0.1 To Station 4.2

Forward section of Privateer fuselage contained teardrop-shaped ventral well for extendable radar. Provision was made for an astrodome aft of the forward upper turret, instead of on top of the nose, where some Liberator pilots complained of restricted visibility caused by the bulging astrodome.

Sent back to Convair for installation of the single tail and new-style engine packages after flying with a twin tail, the number one XPB4Y-2 Privateer was photographed in January 1944. (Todd Hackbarth collection)

Betty 7

Emily 2

Zeke 1

Jake 2

Tess 6

Seventeen additional enemy aircraft of several types were destroyed on the ground by VPB-115; five others, both in the air and on the ground, were listed as probably destroyed, and an even dozen Japanese aircraft were carried on VPB-115 records as being damaged in the air or on the ground. In perspective, VPB-115 lost one PB4Y-1 to probable enemy action, four to operational mishaps, and two as a result of Japanese bombing, for a total of seven stricken Liberators.[2]

The loss of these Liberators con-

tributed to the Squadron's listing of 10 men missing due to probable enemy action; 12 missing due to operational causes; one confirmed dead due to operational causes; three killed as a result of a Japanese bombing raid; and seven Squadron members wounded in action.[3] Squadron contacts with enemy surface ships totaled 725 Japanese vessels sighted; 114 attacked; 46 destroyed; nine probably destroyed; and 44 damaged. Vessels sighted ranged from troop barges and river steamers to battleships; the largest ships attacked by the Squadron's Liberators were five destroyer escorts, three of which suffered damage.[4]

The Squadron's contribution to

the prosecution of the Pacific war was important; the vast watery expanses over which Japan had tossed a sometimes-fragile net of domain depended on shipping for survival. Any disruptions in Japanese ship movements chipped

Mischief Maker III of VPB-115 boasted six downed Japanese aircraft and five ships when this snapshot was made. (Henry Harmon collection)

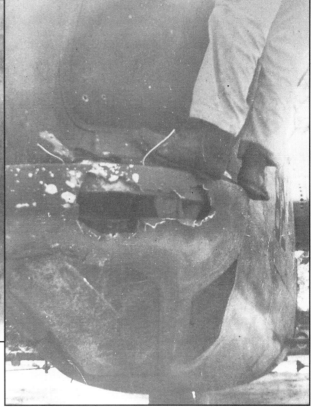

The bow turret and waist of Paul Bruneau's PB4Y-1 were ripped by Japanese shore batteries at Satawan on 19 May 1944. (Henry Harmon collection)

away at that country's war-making capabilities by scuttling combat-bound equipment and soldiers, as well as possibly sinking resources intended to reach Japan.

Following VPB-115's combat tour, Squadron commander J.R. Compton passed several recommendations on to the Pacific Fleet air forces commander. Compton observed: "Low-level bombing with drops made by pilot using cockpit 'pickle' and 'seaman's eye' judgment proved to be (the) most productive form of attack on shipping…" Compton said a string of three to five bombs spaced at minimum interval was normally used. He urged additional training emphasis be given to low-level bombing against towed targets.[5]

Though the branches of America's armed forces fought against a common enemy, some frictions arose between the Navy and the Air Force, perhaps merely the evidence of procedural differences. Whatever the origin, VPB-115's skipper Compton felt compelled to note in his post-tour report: "It is felt that much of the difficulty experienced in procurement of spares and parts for the PB4Y would be eliminated if the supply program for this aircraft were integrated and administered by naval aviation supply activities in the area, rather than depending, as at present, on Army Air Forces supply source." Compton also noted his Liberators had "grown old before their time" while in combat because the squadron operated from a total of six bases, only one of which had adequate maintenance support capabilities. The other bases could only perform limited maintenance, and Compton noted, "the material condition of aircraft has suffered accordingly."[6]

Among the 18 flight crews origi-

nally fielded by VPB-115 was Crew Four, headed by Lt. Paul J. Bruneau. Bruneau's crew aggressively engaged Japanese aircraft during their patrol sorties, destroying a twin-engine bomber, a single-engine fighter, and three twin-engine transports in aerial engagements, as well as a twin-engine bomber on the ground. During these engagements, Crew Four fought off an attack by three Japanese fighters north of Celebes, and brought their Liberator back.[7]

Gunner Henry B. Harmon, part of Paul Bruneau's vigorous aircrew, recalled: "We had an aggressive aircraft commander (Lt. P.J. Bruneau) and it was pretty well SOP (standard operating procedure) for us to engage aircraft, ships (within reason), or to bomb anything worthwhile that we saw. I think our whole crew thought we were there for that reason."[8]

Circa 1948, a late-production PB4Y-1 Liberator of navy photographic squadron VP-61 cruised over southern California. Enclosed waist windows, typical of late Liberator production, probably used K-6 gun mounts with Bell recoil adaptors and Mk. 9 gunsights. Of interest is extra window on command deck near trailing edge of wing. Postwar red-barred national insignia appear to be painted directly on sea blue finish, without using insignia blue background. (Peter M. Bowers collection)

Paul J. Bruneau recalled the primary mission of VPB-115 was successful reconnaissance. Targets of opportunity could be attacked as long as such attacks did not hamper the main recon mission. Bruneau amplified the definition of targets of opportunity, saying: "'Targets of opportunity' was to be

Retired from the U.S. Coast Guard, this P4Y-2G (G for Coast Guard) number 66230 was stored in Arizona with surplus Douglas Skyraiders.

interpreted to mean any naval or air components, or shore installations, that could be destroyed or seriously damaged with reasonable impunity. The probability of casualties or crippling damage to the aircraft was strictly a judgement call on the part of the patrol plane commander."[9]

Bruneau's crew flew aggressively, but with their survival in mind. A 19 April 1944 search of Satawan involved a run-in from the south, across the waves at 25 feet, followed by a pull-up to 170 feet for a bombing and strafing run. Lieutenant Bruneau then circled, out of range, climbing to 1,000 feet for a photographic run with a K-20 camera over the west end of the runway, followed by a smart dive back to 25 feet, and retirement to the northwest. The crew was pleased to report that jinking and high speed were effective in throwing off the Japanese gunners, none of whom scored any hits on the Liberator.[10]

With VPB-115 squadron commander Lt. Cdr. J.R. Compton on board, Paul Bruneau and his crew launched a 23 April 1944 search mission for a fellow VPB-115 Liberator crew missing from the previous day. The Liberator carried a bomb load, but when a lone Mitsubishi Betty twin-engine bomber was sighted cruising about 4,000 feet above the PB4Y-1, the VPB-115 crew immediately jettisoned the bombs and set the throttles at military power. The PB4Y-1 was climbing to attack the Betty. During much of the ascent, Bruneau kept his Liberator aft and below the enemy bomber to avoid detection. Finally, the larger PB4Y-1 climbed to 14,200 feet to commence a shallow, slow-power glide

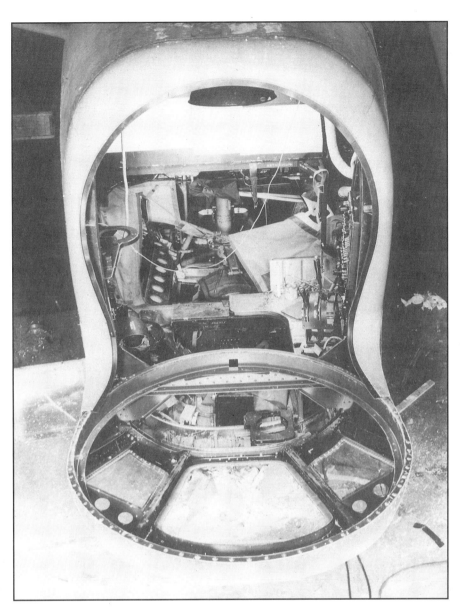

Early U.S. Navy PB4Y-1 BuAer No. 32048 traded its greenhouse nose for an Erco bow turret at North Island Naval Air Station, California, in May 1943. Opened nose shows early-style inwardly-opening nosewheel doors, and interior furnishings. (Chuck Hansen collection)

to an attack position on the Betty's starboard quarter at about 12,000 feet. With Compton in one of the pilots' seats giving direction, Bruneau closed the distance between his bomber and the Japanese bomber. Bruneau's gunners were reminded over interphone by Lieutenant Commander Compton to hold their fire until closure was achieved, and to concentrate their streams of .50-caliber fire

on the Betty's righthand engine, the cockpit, and the potentially troublesome tail gun emplacement.[11]

The Japanese bomber crew appeared unaware they were being stalked by the four-engine Liberator until Bruneau's top turret gunner J.W. Furey, bow turret gunner A.P. Wiswell, and ball turret gunner L.W. Edwards blasted the

More subtle countershading is evident on Privateer with Motor Products nose turret. This example also tested tail radar in a sphere by the tail turret. (Peter M. Bowers collection)

bomber from a range of between 400 and 500 yards. Three single bursts from the Betty's 20-millimeter tail cannon were noted before the Liberator's gunners torched the enemy bomber's starboard engine. The engine subsequently ripped free of the Betty; other pieces of the Mitsubishi were shed as the Japanese aircraft entered a steep dive; then momentarily leveled off before spiraling to an explosive crash into the sea. The incident's after-action report unemotionally noted: "There was no possibility of survivors."[12]

The mathematics of the chase and downing of the Betty by Paul Bruneau's crew showed the enemy bomber to be cruising at about 150 knots. The big Liberator's four R-1830 engines allowed an indicated airspeed of about 130 knots in the climb behind the unwary Betty. The climb and pursuit were drawn out

over 28 minutes and about 60 miles. The closest Bruneau's Liberator came to the Betty was about 50 yards, according to the report.[13]

Paul Bruneau and crew capitalized on the single-ship missions often flown by Navy Liberators to engage in offensive air-to-air combat like the downing of the Betty, rather than merely manning the Liberator's guns defensively. But Bruneau's gunners could defend their Liberator well, as they showed on 19 May 1944 while on a mission from Green Island, bombing Satawan shipping at mast-top height. As the Liberator crew watched a single 500-pound bomb from their PB4Y-1 air burst over a Japanese freighter that was part of a four-ship convoy, return fire was largely ineffective. Now out of the west, three Zekes and a Hamp roared in to attack the lone

Liberator. While the Zekes peeled off for gunnery runs, the Hamp released four phosphorous bombs over Bruneau's patrol bomber. One of these exploded in ribbons of white smoke 800 feet directly above the Liberator; two others were 800 yards off to the right, and one burst 800 yards astern. The three Zekes spent some time flying out of range off the starboard bow of the PB4Y-1, initiating only three really serious attacks. In response to the Japanese fighters' obvious roll-ins to attack, Bruneau nosed his Liberator down from about 300 feet to only 50 feet above the water, accelerating sufficiently to put the Zeke in a harmless pass astern the PB4Y-1, out of firing position. Gunner Hank Harmon years later recalled part of the reason for diving to 50 feet was to deny the Japanese fighters the chance to make an attack from overhead, in which the pull-out

would be thwarted by the nearness of the waves. At low level, the fighters were forced to fly lateral pursuit curves. "As they began their run," Harmon remembered, "our pilot would turn into them. This gave our bow, belly, and upper deck turrets close to a head-on shot, instead of a deflection shot." When one Zeke came within reach of Bruneau's gunners, R.D. Shoden in the Erco bow turret and J.W. Furey in the Martin upper turret shared credit for smoking the Mitsubishi fighter. Five men saw the Japanese pilot bail out, and watched as his parachute opened, and his stricken fighter subsequently impacted. After a 20-minute chase by another Zeke, the Japanese flier finally turned back toward Satawan.[14]

Paul Bruneau's crew had flown to Satawan to attack shipping, and the now-ended fighter attacks would not deter them. Bruneau wheeled the Liberator back toward Satawan for two more low-level attacks. Some damage to Japanese shipping was observed, but, in the heat of battle, hard to substantiate. Anti-aircraft fire from the ships was of dubious accuracy, but heavy flak from Japanese shore batteries on Bruneau's last run over Satawan threw off the bomb run, wounded one man in the bomber seriously, and extensively punctured the Liberator. For the first time in VPB-115's combat experience, flak suits showed their worth. Henry Harmon, manning a waist gun, sustained bruises and blisters when flak punched his flak suit. But the energy absorbed by the heavy flak suit may have saved his life. Up in the bow turret, gunner R.D. Shoden sat on a flak suit that took punishment when 40-millimeter flak ripped into the turret, halting its rotation by damaging the azimuth gear. An observer, A.L. Stephen, listed as a passenger in the PB4Y-1, suffered the worst injuries when 40-millimeter fragments riddled his torso, arms, and legs.[15]

After a takeoff delayed because of the previous night's enemy bombing, Bruneau's crew left Wakde on 9 June 1944 for a routine 800-mile sector patrol. As the PB4Y-1 droned on, gunner R.D. Shoden, looking out from an open waist hatch, spied two Japanese Tess twin-engine transport airplanes about 2,000 feet below the Liberator's cruising altitude of 9,000 feet. Bruneau turned to make one long pass over both enemy targets. The bow, top, waist, and tail gunners all fired at the first Tess, which

Variations in PB4Y-2 camouflage schemes include spotty white countershading under wings, tail, and Erco blisters, photographed on Convair San Diego flightline. (SDAM)

Early PB4Y-2s may have been painted olive drab and gray instead of the hues of blue, gray, and white seen in combat. (Todd Hackbarth collection)

suffered hits in the wing roots, fuselage, and engines that caused it to burn, and crash explosively into the sea. The second Tess took hits from the Liberator's top and bow gunners, and followed the first Tess to a violent demise in the ocean. The Liberator crew noted no return fire from either aircraft. Gunners participating included A.P. Wiswell in the bow turret, Archie R. Hollis in the waist, Richard D. Shoden in the tail turret, and John W. Furey in the top turret. This indicates Bruneau's gunners sometimes switched positions, a practice encouraged by some aircraft commanders to enhance overall gunnery capabilities.[16]

Three days later, Bruneau and crew got another Tess, when an 800-mile sector patrol from Wakde toward the Philippines led them near the Japanese transport. As the Liberator cruised, top turret gunner J.W. Furey caught sight of another aircraft some 11 miles distant. The aircraft proved to be a Tess, about 500 feet higher than the PB4Y-1. From the Japanese transport's abrupt change of course to take up a new heading toward cumulus clouds while diving to pick up speed, Bruneau's crew figured they had been spotted by the enemy. Setting the four PB4Y-1 engines at 45 inches of manifold pressure and 2500 rpm pulled the Liberator along at an indicated airspeed of 210 knots, while in a descent that lost 1,000 feet per minute. Four minutes later, the Tess was overtaken by Bruneau's Liberator.[17]

Only gunner Furey in the Martin top turret could engage the Tess, as the bow turret was inoperative for an ammunition feed jam, and the ball turret was out of action with a defective solenoid. The tail turret could not be brought to bear in a chasing attack. At a distance esti-mated to be 400 yards, Furey cut loose with his machine guns. Immediately an explosion in the Tess blew out cockpit glass as flames whipped back from the belly of the Japanese aircraft. Bruneau's crew watched the Tess enter a steep death spiral, impacting the ocean at an angle of 45 degrees.[18] Paul Bruneau's crew had, collectively, equated the tasks of an ace by downing five enemy aircraft in aggressive actions over the Pacific.

Nearly a half-century after his Pacific Liberator combats, Paul Bruneau was emphatic in his affection for the PB4Y-1: "I loved the old Liberator. It was a magnificent fighting machine and, thank God, could take terrific battle damage and still get us back."[19] Gunner Hank Harmon conveyed similar sentiments: "I really liked the PB4Y-1, except for the fuel system."

Harmon added: "It was a good aircraft, well armed, and could take a lot of punishment. And since it had a long range, it suited our purpose very well. We covered a lot of Pacific Ocean on our patrols."[20]

If Paul Bruneau and his crew racked up more aircraft kills than some of their fellow PB4Y airmen, the Bruneau crew still reflects basic traits common to many Navy Liberator fliers: Cooperation, courage, and creativity under fire.

VPB-115 LIBERATOR ROSTER

From individual crew logs as well as transcriptions of squadron histories, the following Bureau of Aeronautics (BuAer) serial numbers have been identified as VPB-115 PB4Y-1 Liberators: 32082, 32150, 32159, 32162, 32165, 32168, 32169, 32176, 32178, 32182, 32215, 32217, 32220, 32222, 32225, 32238, 32243, 32268, 32274, 32298, 32301, 32302, 32304, 38841.

Although the original complement of aircraft assigned to VPB-115 was 12 PB4Y-1s plus three spares, this higher tally of BuAer numbers is possible due to attrition and replacements during the squadron's duty.

VPB-115 Liberator gunner Hank Harmon recalled in 1994 that, "…our aircraft were painted olive drab…". (This matches photos of early Pacific veteran PB4Y-1s; later Navy Liberators wore versions of triple-tone blue and white camouflage.) Harmon's pilot, Paul Bruneau, recalled some VPB-115 Liberators were blue while others were olive drab. It is apparent from the shades of paint in PB4Y-1 photos, plus the recollections of veterans, that some Navy Liberators, especially in the Pacific, entered combat in olive drab camouflage.

POSTWAR TAIL CODES

A two-letter tail code system was employed by many Privateer units (and the few remaining Liberator squadrons) in the post-World War Two U.S. Navy, beginning in 1946. Units and their tail codes included:

BB…VPHL-13, 1946 (ex-VP-115); VP-25, 1948 (Privateers)

BD…VPHL-5, 1946 (ex-VP-143); VP-46 (VPMS-6), 1948; VP-28, circa1949; VP-46, 1950; (Privateers)

CB…VPML-3, 1946 (ex-VP-136); VP-3, 1948; VP-9, 1953; (Privateers)

CF…VP-28 (ex-VPHL-8), 1948; (Privateers)

CH…VP-871, circa 1951-52; VP-19, 1954; (Privateers)

Overall dark blue Privateer (BuAer No. 59888) is fitted with blunt nose cap for ferry flight to Litchfield Park, Arizona, for attachment of nose turret and bombardier's station. (SDAM)

Early version of XPB4Y-2 single tail used higher placement of rudder trim tab and slightly shorter rounded vertical fin cap than did production tails. (Todd Hackbarth collection)

EH...VP-23 (ex-VPHL-3), 1948; VP-56, 1953 (Privateers)

EI... (Privateers)

HA...VPHL-4, 1946 (ex-VP-104); VP-24, 1948 (Privateers)

PB...VJ-61, 1953; (Liberators)

SD...VP-61 (ex-VPP-1), 1948; (Liberators)

XA...VX-1, 1948 (Privateers)

SPLASHING THE LAST PRIVATEER DRONE

Bert Creighton figured he had a new use for the Bullpup pilot-guided air-to-ground missile. If a jet pilot could watch the path described by a Bullpup's two visual cue flares, and make joystick radio inputs to guide the missile to a ground target, why not use the same principle for air-to-air attacks on slow-movers, especially heli-copters? Bert devised his thesis based on the potential, then build-ing, for such combats in Vietnam.

Creighton, then a pilot in Navy Squadron VX-4 at Point Mugu, Calif., persuaded the Navy to arm the smaller variant of the Bullpup (it had a 250-pound warhead) for an air-to-air test against the last QP-4B Privateer drone in service, he recalled in an interview. The normal Bullpup impact fuze was replaced with a proximity fuze for Creighton's test, and he took off in a sporty A-4 Skyhawk jet, generating good-natured jeers from the Privateer drone operators.

The Point Mugu Missile newspa-per put the date of the last Privateer drone loss at January 18, 1964. So confident were the Privateer operators that Creighton would fail, they left a mascot mouse aboard the fiery-red drone bomber that day after ferrying the QP-4B from Point Mugu to San Nicholas Island for the test, he said.

Creighton estimated he was about a mile from the Privateer when he loosed a proximity-fuzed Bullpup toward the red target drone as it flew over the Pacific Ocean. Bullpup tactics required Creighton to hold a fairly steady course behind his launched missile, to enable him to sight its flares in relation to the target, and make radio inputs on a joystick to guide the device to the target. He figured he was at the same altitude as the Privateer when he launched the Bullpup; had he been below the bomber, it might have taxed the missile's rocket motor too much to try to make it climb to its target, since the heavy Bullpup was designed for descending flight to ground targets.

Astounding his critics, Creighton was dead on the money as the

Crashed 6th BG LB-30 number AL 623 shows the practice of painting the lower halves of the vertical tails white over gray on some sea-search LB-30s. Fixed wind deflector ahead of waist window was modification added to many USAAF LB-30s; B-24s introduced extend-able deflectors. (Edward I. Harrington collection)

Bullpup roared over the top of the Privateer and detonated with a force that fatally crippled the four-engine bomber. "It just blew the propellers off it and it flipped over on its back and spun down," Bert remembered.

In the end, Bullpups were not adopted as air-to-air weapons. The drawbacks of keeping the launch aircraft steady behind the flying missile were unhealthy in most combat situations, Creighton explained. "Fire-and-forget" air-to-air missiles with their own internal tar-get seeking devices were the norm.

And Bert Creighton acknowl-edged he felt badly about the mouse fatality that day over the Pacific Missile Test Range, when the last Privateer in Navy service was splashed.

[1] Transcription by VPB-115 veterans, of VPB-115 Report of Combat Zone Operations, dated 7 November 1944, from Commander Patrol-Bombing Squadron One Hundred Fifteen, to Commander Air Force, Pacific Fleet. [2] *Ibid.* [3] *Ibid.* [4] *Ibid.* [5] *Ibid.* [6] *Ibid.* [7] Extracted from transcription of VPB-115 official war diary. [8] Letter, Henry Harmon to Frederick A. Johnsen, 11 January 1994. [9] Letter, Paul J. Bruneau to Frederick A. Johnsen, 31 December 1993. [10] Transcription of narrative extract from VB-115 Aircraft Action Report #9, 19 April 1944. [11] Transcripted narra-tive extract from VB-115 Aircraft Action Report #14, 23 April 1944. [12] *Ibid.* [13] *Ibid.* [14] Transcripted narrative extract from VB-115 Aircraft Action Report #26, 19 May 1944; also, letter from Henry Harmon to Frederick A. Johnsen, 11 January 1994. [15] *Ibid.* [16] Transcript of narrative extract from VB-115 Aircraft Action Report #33, 9 June 1944. [17] Transcribed narrative extract from VB-115 Aircraft Action Report #35, 12 June 1944. [18] *Ibid.* [19] Letter, Paul J. Bruneau to Frederick A. Johnsen, 31 December 1993. [20] Letter, Henry B. Harmon to Frederick A. Johnsen, 11 January 1994.

PB4Y-2B was designation applied to Privateers fitted to carry and launch a Bat radar-direct-ed bomb from each wing. (Todd Hackbarth collection)

APPENDIX

The following list represents C-87s, C-109s, and B-24s assigned to the India China Division, Air Transport Command (ICDATC) as of 31 May 1945. Following the end of hostilities, this Division ended its Hump operations in November 1945; its other missions were taken over by ATC's Pacific and North African Divisions in 1946. Some B-24s were used in this region for gasoline hauling, as were the specially-designated and modified C-109s. (Typical abbreviations: ASC=Air Service Command; HQ=Headquarters)

CALL SIGN	TYPE	SERIAL NUMBER	ASSIGNED	CALL SIGN	TYPE	SERIAL NUMBER	ASSIGNED
228A	C-87	39228	Jorhat	1372	B-24	41372	Tezpur
229A	C-87	39229	ASC	1390	C-109	51390	ASC
234B	C-109	49234	1300 Atchd Gaya	1420	C-109	51420	Shamshernagar
239A	C-87	39239	Jorhat	1424	C-109	51424	1300 Atchd Gaya
240A	C-87	39240	ASC	1426	B-24	41426	Tezpur
274A	C-87	39274	Jorhat	1429	C-109	51429	Shamshernagar
459A	B-24	42459	Tezpur	1434	B-24	41434	Tezpur
660A	C-109	49660	Jorhat	1659	C-109	51659	ASC
684A	C-109	49684	Shamshernagar	1676	C-109	51676	1300 Atchd Gaya
720A	C-109	49720	Shamshernagar	1684	C-109	51684	1300 Atchd Gaya
857A	B-24	50857	Tezpur	1712	C-109	51712	Kurmitola
986A	B-24	40986	Tezpur	1721	C-109	51721	Shamshernagar
987A	B-24	40987	Tezpur	1756	C-109	51756	Shamshernagar
0231	B-24	40231	Tezpur	1782	C-109	51782	Shamshernagar
0274	B-24	40274	Tezpur	1788	C-109	51788	Shamshernagar
0548	C-87	30548	Jorhat	1792	C-109	51792	Kurmitola
0559	C-87	30559	Jorhat	1793	C-109	51793	Shamshernagar
0560	C-87	30560	ASC	1810	C-109	51810	1300 Atchd Gaya
0581	C-87	30581	Jorhat	1817	C-109	51817	Shamshernagar
0589	C-87	30589	Jorhat	1846	C-109	51846	ASC
0591	C-87	30591	ASC	1849	C-109	51849	ASC
0604	C-87	30604	Jorhat	1854	C-109	51854	Shamshernagar
0610	C-87	30610	Jorhat	1876	C-109	51876	Shamshernagar
0613	C-87	30613	Jorhat	1877	C-109	51877	1300 Atchd Gaya
0621	C-87	30621	Jorhat	1883	C-109	51883	Jorhat
0812	B-24	40812	Tezpur	1893	C-109	51893	Shamshernagar
0816	B-24	40816	Tezpur	1895	B-24	11895	Headquarters ASC
0855	B-24	40855	Tezpur	1904	C-109	51904	Shamshernagar
0857	B-24	40857	Tezpur	2014	C-109	52014	Shamshernagar
0862	B-24	40862	1300 Atchd Gaya	2020	C-109	52020	Kurmitola
0951	B-24	50951	Tezpur	2023	C-109	52023	Shamshernagar
0988	B-24	40988	Tezpur	2049	C-109	52049	Shamshernagar
0989	B-24	40989	Tezpur	2116	B-24	42116	Tezpur
0994	B-24	40994	Tezpur	2251	B-24	42251	Tezpur
1054	B-24	41054	1300 Atchd Gaya	2252	B-24	42252	Tezpur
1125	B-24	41125	HQ, AAF IBT	2258	B-24	42258	Tezpur
1168	B-24	41168	ASC	2259	B-24	42259	Tezpur
1169	B-24	41169	351 Kurmitola	2275	B-24	42275	Tezpur
1180	B-24	41180	1300 Atchd Gaya	2453	B-24	42453	Tezpur
1222	B-24	41222	Tezpur	2454	B-24	42454	Tezpur
1223	B-24	41223	Tezpur	2458	B-24	42458	Tezpur

APPENDIX

CALL SIGN	TYPE	SERIAL NUMBER	ASSIGNED	CALL SIGN	TYPE	SERIAL NUMBER	ASSIGNED
2978	C-87	52978	ASC	9218	C-87	39218	Jorhat
2980	C-87	52980	Jorhat	9227	C-87	39227	ASC
2982	C-87	52982	ASC	9232	C-87	39232	Jorhat
4161	C-87	24161	Jorhat	9234	C-87	39234	ASC
4244	B-24	24244	1300 Atchd Gaya	9235	C-87	39235	Jorhat
7255	C-87	107255	ASC	9238	C-87	39238	Jorhat
7265	C-87	107265	ASC	9241	C-87	39241	ASC
8685	B-24	78685	Tezpur	9242	C-87	39242	Jorhat
8686	B-24	78686	Tezpur	9247	C-87	39247	Jorhat
8688	B-24	78688	Tezpur	9263	C-87	39263	Jorhat
8690	B-24	78690	Tezpur	9264	C-87	39264	Jorhat
8693	B-24	78693	Tezpur	9266	C-87	39266	ASC
8792	C-109	48792	Kurmitola	9267	C-87	39267	Jorhat
8877	C-109	48877	Shamshernagar	9268	C-87	39268	Jorhat
8883	C-109	48883	Shamshernagar	9269	C-87	39269	Jorhat
8888	C-109	48888	Shamshernagar	9270	C-87	39270	Jorhat
8890	C-109	48890	Shamshernagar	9272	C-87	39272	Jorhat
8892	C-109	48892	Shamshernagar	9273	C-87	39273	Jorhat
8948	C-109	48948	Shamshernagar	9275	C-87	39275	Jorhat
8979	C-109	48979	Shamshernagar	9280	C-87	39280	Jorhat
8999	C-109	48999	Shamshernagar	9282	C-87	39282	Jorhat
9001	C-109	49001	Shamshernagar	9283	C-87	39283	Jorhat
9007	C-109	49007	Kurmitola	9284	C-87	39284	Jorhat
9008	C-109	49008	Kurmitola	9288	C-87	39288	Jorhat
9009	C-109	49009	Kurmitola	9290	C-87	39290	Jorhat
9017	C-109	49017	Shamshernagar	9291	C-87	39291	Jorhat
9018	C-109	49018	Jorhat	9292	C-87	39292	Jorhat
9019	C-109	49019	Kurmitola	9294	C-87	39294	Jorhat
9020	C-109	49020	Shamshernagar	9296	C-87	39296	Jorhat
9022	C-109	49022	ASC	9297	C-87	39297	Jorhat
9023	C-109	49023	Jorhat	9298	C-87	39298	Jorhat
9031	C-109	49031	Kurmitola	9302	C-109	49302	Jorhat
9034	C-109	49034	Kurmitola	9351	C-109	49351	Kurmitola
9035	C-109	49035	1300 Gaya	9352	C-109	49352	Shamshernagar
9040	C-109	49040	Shamshernagar	9353	C-109	49353	Jorhat
9057	C-109	49057	Shamshernagar	9354	C-109	49354	Shamshernagar
9059	C-109	49059	Shamshernagar	9554	B-24	49554	Tezpur
9063	C-109	49063	Shamshernagar	9574	B-24	49574	Tezpur
9065	C-109	49065	Shamshernagar	9604	B-24	49604	Tezpur
9067	C-109	49067	Shamshernagar	9615	C-109	49615	Jorhat
9071	C-109	49071	Shamshernagar	9621	C-109	49621	Shamshernagar
9075	C-109	49075	Kurmitola	9628	C-109	49628	Jorhat
9077	C-109	49077	Shamshernagar	9662	C-109	49662	Kurmitola
9079	C-109	49079	Shamshernagar	9704	C-109	49704	Jorhat
9184	C-109	49184	Shamshernagar	9715	C-109	49715	Shamshernagar
9216	C-87	39216	Jorhat	9723	C-109	49723	Shamshernagar
9217	C-87	39217	ASC				

SIGNIFICANT DATES

30 MARCH 1939: Contract signed by Consolidated Aircraft and Army Air Corps for prototype and mock-up B-24.

29 DECEMBER 1939: First flight of XB-24 at San Diego, California.

17 JANUARY 1941: First flight of LB-30A variant.

JUNE 1941: First B-24A delivered to USAAF; first British Coastal Command Liberator Is begin patrols.

7 DECEMBER 1941: First USAAF combat Liberator loss is B-24A 40-2370, bombed by Japanese at Hickam Field.

19 DECEMBER 1941: Rollout of first of nine B-24Cs, which set the style for the much-produced B-24D.

22 JANUARY 1942: First B-24D delivered, at San Diego.

1 MAY 1942: First B-24D assembled at Consolidated Fort Worth, Texas, plant accepted by USAAF.

11-12 JUNE 1942: HALPRO B-24Ds make raid on Ploesti; foretaste of things to come, the HALPRO raid is first USAAF land-based strategic bombing mission of any significance in Europe.

1 SEPTEMBER 1942: USAAF accepts first Ford-built B-24 from Willow Run.

OCTOBER 1942: Marine Squadron VMD-254s PB4Y-1s sent to Espiritu Santo for Pacific reconnaissance.

9 OCTOBER 1942: First B-24 Eighth Air Force mission, flown by 93rd Bomb Group to Lille, France.

29 JANUARY 1943: XB-41 escort Liberator delivered to USAAF for evaluation.

6 MARCH 1943: First flight of B-24ST (Single Tail), later evolved as XB-24K.

MAY 1943: Navy places contract with Convair for PB4Y-2.

11 JUNE 1943: First AT-22 Liberator flight engineer trainer accepted by USAAF; five built, similar to C-87s.

30 JUNE 1943: First B-24H (first production Liberator with nose turret) delivered from Ford Willow Run, Michigan, plant. Some North American-built B-24Gs have nose turrets, but this H-model precedes them chronologically.

JULY 1943: First four F-7 photo mapping Liberators (following XF-7 test project in January) converted by Lockheed in Dallas, Texas; these four deploy to the Pacific in December 1943. Total F-7 conversions number 215, including a temporary conversion of a B-24E.

AUGUST 1943: U.S. Navy assumes antisubmarine duties from USAAF, including Liberator mission.

1 AUGUST 1943: B-24Ds totaling 177 aircraft launch mass low-level Ploesti oilfield attack.

31 AUGUST 1943: Convair San Diego plant switches from building B-24D to B-24J.

8 SEPTEMBER 1943: USAAF orders conversion of B-24E to XC-109 gasoline hauler; more than 200 C-109 conversions follow, tanking critically-needed gasoline to B-29s in the China-Burma-India Theater, and to forces on the European continent following D-Day.

20 SEPTEMBER 1943: First flight of XPB4Y-2 Privateer (with twin tails).

2 FEBRUARY 1944: XPB4Y-2 re-delivered to Navy with single-tail configuration.

AUGUST 1944: By mid-month, Consolidated San Diego and Ford have converted to production of B-24L; Consolidated Fort Worth continues building J-models to year end; Douglas and North American quit B-24 production during July and November 1944, respectively.

AUGUST 1944: C-87 production ends at 286 aircraft; a few other non-factory C-87-type conversions are also made.

SEPTEMBER 1944: USAAF tallies operational strength of 6,043 B-24s—the peak number of Liberators attained by the Air Force.

OCTOBER 1944: B-24M introduced.

NOVEMBER 1944: XB-24N single-tail variant (44-48753) built by Ford delivered to USAAF.

JANUARY 1945: PB4Y-2 Privateer achieves operational status with squadrons VPB-118 and -119 at Tinian and Midway. Other Privateer squadrons will follow in Pacific combat.

JANUARY 1945: Last PB4Y-1 (comparable to B-24M) delivered to U.S. Navy.

23 APRIL 1945: VPB-109 Privateer launches two Bat radar-guided bombs against Japanese shipping in Balikpapan Harbor, Borneo; first combat with World War Two's only automatic-homing missile.

30 MAY 1945: First YB-24N, 44-52053, accepted by USAAF.

31 MAY 1945: Cessation of B-24 Liberator production.

OCTOBER 1945: Last of 740 PB4Y-2 Privateers delivered.

29 NOVEMBER 1945: XB-24K scrapped.

12 MAY 1946: Original Liberator prototype, now designated XB-24B, dropped from Air Force inventory for scrapping.

17 SEPTEMBER 1947: Air Force reclassifies B-24 from heavy bomber to light bomber, reflecting influx of larger B-29s and B-36s. Last seven Liberators to return from a war theater are ferried from Alaska earlier this year.

MARCH 1948: RY-3 number JT973, "Rockliffe Ice Wagon," retired by Royal Canadian Air Force; other RY-3 transports retired earlier.

8 APRIL 1950: PB4Y-2 Privateer from Navy squadron VP-26 shot down by Soviet fighter over the Baltic.

18 MAY 1959: B-24D arrives at Air Force Museum, Wright-Patterson AFB, after ferry flight from Davis-Monthan AFB, Arizona.

18 JANUARY 1964: Last QP-4B Privateer drone in U.S. Navy shot down in test off Point Mugu, California, ending American military Liberator/Privateer use.